Copyright @ 2016 Datche Press

All rights are reserved.

No part of this publication may be reproduced, stored in a retrieval

System or transmitted in any form or by any means, electronic,

Mechanical, photocopying, recording or otherwise, without

prior permission of Datche Press

ACKNOWLEGEMENTS

I lovingly dedicate this book to my awesome husband whose company I enjoy and who have made me grow stronger spiritually and academically, trusting and supporting me in all areas of my life. Haimdat, I love you profoundly and always!

To my loving parents, Krishna Sammy and Radica Angela Eliah, whose support throughout my life has been exceptional, complete and a spiritual blessing from the Universe. I wouldn't be who I am today without your constant dedication, love and affection for me. I am especially grateful for the joy and laughter that you have enriched my life with. I love you both now and forever! To my talented and amazing brother Krisna, I respect you for being able to stay on purpose no matter your environment and for motivating me to live a purposeful life.

To Lorenzo Sewanan, you have inspired me ever since my childhood and for that I am grateful.

To my Suriname Hindu Guyanese Cultural Organization (SHGCO) family. I wouldn't be complete, without your love and support. You are all simply the best family I could have in my life. Thanks!!

To His Excellency Ambassador Keith George of Guyana to Suriname. My dear brother and friend, Haimdat and I are honored to have you in our lives. Thank you for everything!

To Shalini, Ian and Indira, I love you all!

Change Your Blueprint Through Journaling

Mastering your Inner Happiness through Finding your Purpose in your Day to Day Life with your Blueprint Journal

The simplest, most effective thing you can practice every day to feel happier, alive and staying on purpose is to do your dailies!

I believe passionately in the power of ideas to change attitudes, lives and ultimately, the world, but exclusively the self.

MINACHE ELIAH-SAWH

Change Your Blueprint Through Journaling

Mastering your Inner Happiness through Finding your Purpose in your Day to Day Life with your Blueprint Journal

MINACHE ELIAH-SAWH

THIS PAGE IS LEFT INTENTIONALLY BLANK

DEDICATION

I dedicate this book to the Universe for all its guidance and eternal blessings. You have been a constant presence in my life, teaching me how to stay on purpose by being in the moment and listening with my heart, fulfilling my inner most desires and trusting my intuition and smiling with me along the way.

To my Heavenly Father, Divine Mother, Lord Jesus Christ, Bhagavan Krishna, Babaji, Lahiri Mahasaya, Sri Yukteswarji, Paramahansa Yogananda and saints of all religions, I humbly bow to you all.

May Thy love shine forever on the sanctuary of my devotion, may I awaken Thy love in all hearts. I thank you for your blessings in manifesting this book on Blueprint journaling.

My heart has grown so much with all your Divine love and your blissful presence.

To lifelong learners and doers, you are changing the world every day by changing your thoughts. What you become as a result of daily celebration and introspection is the measure of your progress, your thought patterns and your potential.

To Savitri Sawh I couldn't have found the answer to my prayers without the love and affection that you have showered on me.

ARE YOU CONSTANTLY THINKING OF NEW WAYS TO IMPROVE YOUR WAY OF ...?

YES ⬤ NO ⬤

EVER FEEL LIKE YOU COULD DO ANYTHING – IF ONLY YOU KNEW WHAT IT WAS AND HAD NO FEAR OF LIVING YOUR LIFE TO YOUR HEART'S CONTENT?

YES ⬤ NO ⬤

ARE YOU ONE OF THOSE PEOPLE WHO WON'T SETTLE FOR AN AVERAGE LIFE?

YES ⬤ NO ⬤

ARE YOU READY TO SPEND TIME WITH YOUR DAILY BLUEPRINT JOURNAL TO HELP YOU GAIN CLARITY AT THE PERFECT MOMENT WHEN YOU NEED IT?

YES ⬤ NO ⬤

ARE YOU READY TO STEP OUT OF LIMITING BELIEFS AND ACCESS YOUR OWN GREATEST POTENTIAL?

YES ⬤ NO ⬤

DO YOU GET THAT CONSTANT NAGGING FEELING TO ACHIEVE YOUR HIGHEST PURPOSE IN THIS LIFE?

YES ⬤ NO ⬤

If you've answered "yes" to any of these questions, welcome to

<u>Change Your Blueprint Through Journaling</u>

You are about to step into the light of your dazzling brilliance!!!

Embrace and live your life with Passion and Purpose.

Discover your Purpose!

Master your Relationships!

Become the best you!!

Live each present moment completely and the future will take care of itself. Fully enjoy the wonder and beauty of each instant. Practice the presence of peace. The more you do that, the more you will feel the presence of that power in your life.

You are the master

Of the moments

Of your life.

PARAMAHANSA YOGANANDA

THIS PAGE IS LEFT INTENTIONALLY BLANK

CONTENTS

I. INTRODUCTION   **1**

II. BECOMING CONSCIOUS   **7**
When we expand our thinking and beliefs, our love flows freely.

III. DHARMA DISCOVERIES   **13**
One's essential duty; right action; one's higher purpose in life.

IV. DISSOLVING BARRIERS   **19**
You can create any life you want; the Power is within you.

V. AFFIRMATIVE JOURNALING   **23**
The minute we make an intention, we create it instantaneously.

VI. ULTIMATE PURPOSE OF LIFE   **31**
Achieving your Ultimate purpose of life is to stay on purpose.

VII.	THE JOURNALING ROUTINE	39
VIII.	DAILY AFFIRMATIONS	43
IX.	PRACTICE BEING THANKFUL	47
X.	VISUALIZING YOUR PERFECT DAY	51
XI.	BE KIND WHENEVER POSSIBLE	55
XII.	STAYING ON TRACK WITH YOUR PURPOSE	63
XIII.	YOUR THOUGHTS & IDEAS	69
XIV.	KEEP YOUR VISION IN FRONT OF YOU	73
XV.	ASK! CREATE! MANIFEST!	77
XVI.	CHANGE YOUR BLUEPRINT JOURNALING	83

I. INTRODUCTION

All life is an experiment. The more experiments you create the better.

Change Your Blueprint Through Journaling!

Your Blueprint consists of all your subconscious beliefs, which is a combination of your thoughts, feelings and actions, that is, hardwired in you until you are ready to make positive changes. Your Blueprint is the rulebook your subconscious mind uses to decide how to interpret and interact with people and events in your life. Your Blueprint that was formed from childhood onwards rules your day to day life and the actions you have taken. Many people live their lives by doing the same thing over and over and keep expecting different results, not wanting to make the necessary changes. I have observed that the average person does not do what he wishes to do, but does what he is accustomed to do. This is why some people find it difficult to step out of their comfort zone and make changes in their lives. For example, you might know someone who have kept their job for 30 years, doing the same task each and every day. Or perhaps you may come across someone who is adventurous, stepping out of their comfort zone and grappling with the challenges that comes with life and replacing limiting Blueprint behaviors and or habits with new ones. Similarly, it is also difficult for a mean person to be good and kind. It is just as unthinkable for an honorable person to behave unkindly.

Our Blueprint behaviors are automatically stored in our subconscious mind. We give our behavior the initial use of will power and the determined effort required to behave a specific way.

The Blueprint that we pick up from a young age have been running the entirety of our life. We live in a world that thrives on certain Blueprint behaviors and hence we are unwilling or fear changing our Blueprint for the better. I wrote <u>Change Your Blueprint Through Journaling</u> in an attempt to inspire you to make a new determination to improve your life. You can create and renew your life by being systematic in journaling for an entire year. I urge you to use <u>Change Your Blueprint Through Journaling</u> to master your inner happiness, finding your purpose in your day to day life and staying the course!

A journaling routine has been created for you; carry it through, and you will find how much happier you will be. You have no greater friend or no greater enemy than yourself. If you befriend yourself, you will accomplish much. Nothing detrimental that happens can affect you unless you sanction it.

You are the creator of your good or bad Blueprints. Thus till the soil of your conditioned mind with discipline and sow the seeds of will power to create a changed Blueprint to improve your life and achieve success through journaling. To see the changes and to start living a purposeful life you must be patient in cultivating and mastering or perhaps successfully inputting tremendous amounts of effort exerted over many hours to mastery in a positive Blueprint behavior and step of your comfort zone, while you continuously keep letting go of the cultivated childhood negative Blueprints.

What we give out we get back. Do you agree?

INTRODUCTION

What is your Blueprint truth above all truths? Be honest with yourself and describe your overarching Blueprint truth.

How do you do connect with your higher self? Think.

Do you know your purpose? Are you living an average life? Think, change, write…

I often feel that deep within, we know what our potential is and what our true purpose is, but sometimes we allow the adapted Blueprint fear to take hold of our true meaning to being happy and in celebrating our wins and happiness, daily.

We allow the lack mentality to step in and over take what we deeply want to achieve, that is, to create our abundant life by changing our Blueprint patterns. So what we do, and we do this is so well because we are Blueprinted in our decision, we constantly keep moving backwards with our limitations and our self-sabotaging beliefs. We know that we are going in the wrong direction, but it feels as if we are blind folded allowing ourselves to consistently move backwards. Until we get up and get into action with our Blueprint journal we may not see the results of our life's purpose.

When we expand our thinking and beliefs, our love flows freely. When we contract, we shut ourselves off.

"Those who don't believe in magic will never find it."

—Roald Dahl

To find ourselves without truly believing in the power of our potential is like trying to tether a cloud. Living a life full of purpose is a state of mind that we are powerful beings and we

CHANGE YOUR BLUEPRINT THROUGH JOURNALING

have the will power to step out of the Blueprint beliefs that has been keeping us behind.

Believe in the magic and you shall find it everywhere abundantly.

You still have to do the work in the real world. The Blueprint Journal will guide you along in your daily routine and making the journaling technique an act of free will and not habit.

Thoughts saturated with sincerity, conviction, faith and intuition are like highly explosive vibration bombs, which when set off, shatters the rocks of difficulties and create the Blueprint change desired.

You probably have heard of 'visualize your vision to reality,' or 'write what you want, and it will happen.' You might have tried it, and it did not always work. I know, I have tried those techniques many times and they did not always work for me either, that is, until I was taught the secret to making it happen a lot more. It is the magic of intention, drive, energy and action.

To make something happen or to create something, according to the Newtonian Law of Physics, requires work. To do work, you need to apply a force at a specific rate over a period of time. In order to apply a force, you need to input great amounts of energy in a certain direction and <u>will it</u>, with all your intention. To do so, avoid thinking unpleasant thoughts, watch what you say and the amount of energy you say it with. Sincere thoughts become sincere vision. Sincere vision when repeated in the mind's eye becomes a clear vision, so over powering that this is sure to move the Cosmic Vibratory force to render aid with any positive vision. Believe in your Vision and have no doubts. Cast all doubts away,

INTRODUCTION

otherwise arrow of your attention will be deflected from its mark. As you visualize your intentions, your attitude should align with strong willpower, devotion and understanding.

Step out of your limiting beliefs and live the life you were meant to live.

Ignite your passion with your Blueprint journal!!!

Use your Blueprint Journal Daily.

Continue to amaze the world.

Change your old ways.

Be inspired to Change your Blueprint!

We all have a purpose of some kind to fulfill, why not fulfill it in this life?

I am willing to form and create my Blueprint by seeing my life's purpose and creating a strong will power to see good in everything and in seeing all of my good to manifest through my changes.

"From joy I came.
For joy I live.
And in sacred joy
I shall melt again."
— Paramahansa Yogananda

CHANGE YOUR BLUEPRINT THROUGH JOURNALING

This day shall be the best day of my life. Today I will start with a new determination and will power.

A CHANGE IS WISER FOR MY BLUNDERS

Frame me into an improved thought that I was yesterday

Provide me the command to love without reservation

Lay down my old Blueprints of great decisions

A Change is wiser for my blunders

A cooler side of the pillow

Someone to get up on the left side of the bed

Strength to care for more human than myself

Love yourself, but others more

All of this power resides in you

Stop asking for it

Take it and shape up

Make yourself the best self

Alright frame

You have seen thus far what changes are necessary.

— Minache Eliah-Sawh

II. BECOMING CONSCIOUS

Excellence is an art won by training and habituation. We do not act rightly because we have virtue or excellence, but we rather have those because we have acted rightly.

"We are what we repeatedly do. Excellence, then, is not an act, but a habit."

— Aristotle

"As we are, so we do; and as we do, so is it done to us; we are the builders of our fortunes."

— Ralph Waldo Emerson

CHANGE YOUR BLUEPRINT THROUGH JOURNALING

Chances are you have come across quotes like the one from Aristotle or perhaps Ralph Waldo Emerson. This should make us want to evaluate our present thought in a spilt second, and think about the things we need to change.

Habits of thought controls one's life. Even if you considered yourself ambitious, chances are you find it difficult to implement a series of new behaviors in your life. You make evident success or failure according to your habitual trend of thought, your Blueprint.

You alone have the ability to know your strongest thought, whether it is a success or failure thought? If your mind is regularly in a negative state, rarely a positive thought, then this is insufficient to attract your highest purpose, or even to gain your success at any moment.

Let us shatter our world this moment by accepting that we can change our Blueprint and create an amazing life by changing our thoughts and living in this moment to our highest potential.

This is the moment we are living. This is the moment we are feeling. This is the moment we are experiencing. So why not create the best of everything in this moment.

What we are doing is laying the groundwork for tomorrow. So this is the moment to make the decision. We can't do anything tomorrow, and yesterday is past. We can only do this today. What is important is what we are choosing to think, believe, and say right now.

BECOMING CONSCIOUS

'Beliefs are like roots'...you wouldn't water the leaves of a tree, the leaves are like our knowledge, still important, but first we have to change the beliefs, and then the appropriate knowledge will reveal itself.

When we begin to take conscious charge of our thoughts and words, then we have tools that we can use. I know this sounds simple, but remember, the point of power is always in the present moment.

A couple of interesting questions:
- Where do your thoughts come from?
- Why do you think differently from the next person?

Your thoughts originate from the 'files of information' you have in the storage cabinets of your mind. So where does this information come from? It comes from your past programming. That is right; your past conditioning determines every thought that bubbles up in your mind. That's why it's often referred to as the 'conditioned mind'.

The beliefs that make Your Blueprint can be empowering, crippling, or in-between. And while it is possible for people to have subconscious beliefs that is wide ranging, there usually is a common theme. That's why people tend to be either positive or negative in how they view life. How can we change our Blueprint? We all want to have our lives change, to have situations become better and easier, but we do not want to be the ones making the changes. We would prefer that everyone around us change. In order to have this happen, we must change our hardwire Blueprint from the inside. We must change our way of thinking, change our way of speaking, change our way of expressing ourselves. Only then will the outer changes happen.

CHANGE YOUR BLUEPRINT THROUGH JOURNALING

I have always had a stubborn streak. Even now, when I decide to make a change in my life, this stubbornness can come to the surface, and my resistance to changing my thinking is strong. I can temporarily become self-righteous, angry and or withdrawn. Yes, this still goes on. It's one of my hardwired Blueprint. I know that the change is good for me, but the fight I put up with the self is self-sabotaging and the fear that steps in is overpowering, but then I become conscious of the situation at hand and try to understand the process instead of fighting it. This process of transitioning from an unconscious state of being, to conscious state of being is so natural, especially in this particular phase of my life. If you don't create unnecessary resistance you will move through it quite swiftly. The only reason why people resist this natural evolution is out of a lack of understanding of this process, especially the part of deconstruction of negativity that's a part of this transition. There are various ways through which the release happens.

You suddenly have a lot of fear (or fear based thoughts) coming up in you for no reason. Some events happen in your reality that cause negativity to arise in you (basically the negativity that arises is present in you already and the events only help unearth it). You find yourself becoming overly-sensitive to the negativity in your environment. You become starkly aware of your disconnected reality, creating a sense of hopelessness and frustration in you.

Now all of the above conditions are what your mind will consider "horrible", because the last thing you expected (especially after some blissful experience of awakening) was to deal with all the negativity that comes up to be released. Of course, a lot of people do not have any specific 'blissful' moment of awakening, they just start becoming conscious of their fears owning to the

BECOMING CONSCIOUS

accumulated load of negativity in their energy space. Whatever the case, the goal right now would be to move forward towards consciously finding freedom by releasing the negativity rather than sitting in fear of it, wondering what went wrong. Nothing really went wrong, it's just a natural process of coming back to conscious harmony after periods of unconsciousness.

I believe that fear is the opposite of love. This belief is stopping us from unlocking our unlived potential and holding us back from living our purpose.

For us to live our purpose, to get unstuck and to live the life we know WE <u>must</u> conquer fear! However, conquering fear doesn't mean getting rid of fear. We must learn to see fear in a new way. Did you know that there are two types of fear? There's a good kind of fear and a bad kind of fear.

The good fear means we are coming closer to living our purpose. The bad fear means that we are holding back our unlimited potential.

The Blueprint journal is here to assist you to bring to life all the dormant potential within you and help be a voice of encouragement for you to take the leap and find courage. Journaling daily, you will learn the difference between these two types of fear (good vs bad), you will start to take substantial control over your life. And you will have powerful clarity that will help you understand the exact next steps you can take to get unstuck and get about the business of living your purpose.

Life is waiting everywhere, the future is flowering everywhere, but we only see a small part of it and step on much of it with our feet.

CHANGE YOUR BLUEPRINT THROUGH JOURNALING

You are meant to be a wonderful, loving expression of life.

Life is waiting for you to open up to it, to feel worthy of the good it holds for you.

The wisdom and intelligence of the universe is yours to use. Life is here to support you and so I created this awesome journal for you to discover and live your life with true happiness and fulfilling your highest purpose

III. DHARMA DISCOVERIES

The highest Dharma is to recognize the Truth in one's own heart, to fully realize one's True Self.

— Dharma

"You must live in the present, launch yourself on every wave, and find your eternity in each moment. Fools stand on their island of opportunities and look toward another land. There is no other land; there is no other life but this."

— Henry David Thoreau

"Life can be found only in the present moment."

— Thich Nhat Hanh

"We can't do no great things, only small things with great love."

— Mother Teresa

"As we contemplate leaving the morning of our life, where ego has played a commanding role, and entering the afternoon and evening, where meaning and purpose replace ambition and struggle, we may encounter unexpected occurrences that accompany this new direction. It's almost a universal law that we'll experience a fall of some kind. Yet these falls or low points provide the energy we need to move away from ego and into a life of meaning and purpose."   — The Shift

CHANGE YOUR BLUEPRINT THROUGH JOURNALING

Dharma, is the spiritual principle that implies there is purpose to our life. An author has Dharma, a Teacher has a Dharma, a bird has a Dharma, everything has a purpose and when you find yourself living for that purpose, you have found your Dharma. Your Dharma is something that you will live by and rather than constantly using the ego, you will begin to say this is what I am here for. I call it an inner calling, an inner 'ding'.

How do we know what our Dharma is?
Your Dharma is something that you are always connected to. That right action that present itself from moment to moment. It is your divine purpose. It is something that you are aligned with for your entire life, the ego has kept us away from it, but we all have our calling and changing our Blueprint through Journaling can ignite sparks to light up our Divine purpose.

Dharma is much more than one's career or focus of activity in life. Dharma is the unstoppable force of evolution in the cosmos that impels everything forward toward self-awareness. Everyone has a purpose or Dharma. If we didn't, we wouldn't exist at all.

At some point we have all asked ourselves, what is my life's purpose? Why am I here? The constant nagging as to make sense to it all. Our lives, our hurts, our friends, our family, we tend to cling to ideas of what it all might mean.

These crucial questions come from the depths of our true self, which is nudging us to look beyond the world of appearances and discover our inner divinity.

When we're aligned with our Dharma, we tend to feel happy, focused, and fulfilled. Instead of struggling and pushing to make things happen, we live in the flow.
Unexpected opportunities come our way and we have many experiences of our destiny, in which we're able to easily manifest

DHARMA DISCOVERIES

our intentions and desires through the phenomenon of meaningful coincidences.

Do you believe that we were all sent here for a reason and that we all have significance in the world?

Our significant purpose is realizing that we have a duty to fulfill.

Dharma is the essence of your individuality.

As the universal field of pure potentiality manifests as individual expressions, each being is a reflection of the whole and at that same time brings something unique to the world.

This is the essence of Dharma, that everything and everyone has a purpose in life.

CHANGE YOUR BLUEPRINT THROUGH JOURNALING

Your Journey to Discoveries.

What is your purpose?

Are you happy when you look at your life?

How do I know if I'm living my inner happiness?

You lose track of time. Instead of clock watching or thinking about what you'd rather be doing, you're fully immersed in present moment awareness.

You're excited about the unfolding possibilities and the opportunity to serve others as you express your unique gifts and talents.

You don't seek approval, security, or control. Knowing that your true source of abundance and creativity is infinite, you don't get caught up in the ego's archetypical power struggles.

Your chosen activity feels deeply right and natural to you, even when it sometimes challenges your abilities or, conversely, feels monotonous.

You enjoy your relationships with those who share your life and work.

You feel aligned with the evolutionary flow of the universe, regularly experience synchronistic opportunities and encounters that support you in the fulfillment of your intentions and desires.

Our purpose might change from moment to moment. We are not limited by only one right action or one purpose. Life's meaning is to be open to all that comes our way.

DHARMA DISCOVERIES

Keep in mind that finding and living your purpose isn't a one-time effort. Dharma is an ever-evolving process that depends above all on expanding your self-awareness. Sometimes you will feel completely in the flow, living in harmony with the force of evolution on a moment-by-moment basis. Other times when you feel out of balance and constricted, you may be expressing only a small percentage of your Dharma.

The moment we decide things don't have to be a certain way, we create the possibility that they could better than we know to imagine.

Pursue what the heart desires and that is our rightful action. So what new paradigm are we going to create?
Discover your unique talents and begin to express them more in your life.

Think back to that time when you were working and living your life's purpose and having fun at the same time. What were you doing differently and why did it make you feel good? What talents do you have that you can share with the world? Write it here.

_____
_____
_____
_____

Make a list of things that you enjoy doing. Connect to Your will power by changing the things that doesn't apply to your lifestyle and by changing the negative Blueprints into positive ones. Write it here.

_____
_____
_____

CHANGE YOUR BLUEPRINT THROUGH JOURNALING

_____
_____
_____
_____
_____
_____
_____

Who Am I?

_____
_____
_____
_____
_____
_____

You don't need to search the world to find your purpose. The clues lay hidden deep in your heart. Your determination boils down to your unique gifts, which you can share with the world. When you find your true self, you will find love and joy, and you will express that in every thought and action in your life.

IV. DISSOLVING BARRIERS

"I think the reward for conformity is that everyone likes you except yourself."

— Rita Mae Brown

"Love is the energy of life."

— Robert Browning

"Life is too short to wake up with regrets. So love the people who treat you right. Forget about those who don't. Believe everything happens for a reason. If you get a chance, take it. If it changes your life, let it. Nobody said life would be easy, they just promised it would most likely be worth it."

— Paulo Coelho

"I can teach anybody how to get what they want out of life. The problem is that I can't find anybody who can tell me what they want."

— Mark Twain

CHANGE YOUR BLUEPRINT THROUGH JOURNALING

We want to know what is going on inside of us, so we can discern what to let go of. Instead of hiding our pain, we can journal and release it completely by clearing our negative thoughts to positive ones.

It's impossible to live the life you truly want to live without being in tune with what you want and desire. The truth is that your capacity to create an amazing life is unlimited. You can create any life you want; the power is within you.

This isn't some egoistic thought of needing to be the biggest thing in the world; this is a realistic call to action to live at our highest potential by giving your gifts to the world and letting the universe run our lives and determine the outcome.

Consistently, human history shows that many of mankind's core assumptions about the world have been wrong. Let's take a look:

> The world is flat – wrong.
> The Earth is the center of the Universe – wrong.
> Metal can't float – wrong.
> Man can't fly – wrong.
> Going faster than the speed of sound is impossible – wrong.
> Women aren't equal to men – wrong.

What are your core assumptions TODAY that are wrong?
The universe is a place FULL of POTENTIALITY and POSSIBILITIES not just for mankind, but also for us in our daily lives. Just like we have thought some crazy things in the past, in each of our lives we have limiting beliefs that, like the beliefs listed before, are just wrong.

DISSOLVING BARRIERS

What thoughts or excuses do you have about your life that are holding you back?

Here are some common ones:

I'm too fat.
I'm too skinny.
I'm too old.
I'm too young.
I'm under qualified.
I'm over qualified.
I don't have enough time.
I'm not enough.
I'm not worthy.
I don't have enough money.
No one will like this idea.
I will die if I fail.

These beliefs and many more start to come when we do <u>not</u> expand our possibility and step out of our comfort zone. Know that your limiting beliefs and excuses are wrong.

Here's the truth:

You are enough, right now, just as you are. You can schedule your time, find other ways besides money to make it happen. You will

CHANGE YOUR BLUEPRINT THROUGH JOURNALING

fall down and you will fail, but those are just lessons. The only true failure is the failure of not trying.

"The simple things are also the most extraordinary things, and only the wise can see them."
— Paulo Coelho

Your dreams, your desires are REAL and can BE if you take consistent action towards them. Every time we expand, we may be met with limiting beliefs. Take the time to notice the limiting beliefs and journal the opposite beliefs and then just move forward. Let's strengthen our minds to be conditioned to believe empowering thoughts, instead of disempowering thoughts. Let's train our mind and take action over time to prove these empowering thoughts right. What limiting beliefs, excuses and the like are you buying into? Which ones do you want to throw away today and take in a different direction? Are you willing to burn in the fire of your heart's desire for as long as it takes to make it happen? Are you willing to surrender the outcome to the universe?

As always, the action happens over in your journal leave your comment, your excuses and limiting beliefs. Break the barriers that keep holding you back. Change that unwilling mind and conquer your power of your will with your Blueprint journaling techniques. You choose, so choose to live in harmony with what you value and appreciate. You can choose, so choose to be purposeful, persistent and effective

V. AFFIRMATIVE JOURNALING

"True success is overcoming the fear of being unsuccessful."

— Paul Sweeney

"There is only one thing that makes a dream impossible to achieve: the fear of failure."

— Paulo Coelho

Feelings are the magnet when it comes to realizing your dreams and goals.

CHANGE YOUR BLUEPRINT THROUGH JOURNALING

Affirmative journaling is where we write to bridge the gap between our current reality and the desired outcome; whether it's events, goals, feelings, situations or whatever. We write as if these things are already so, including our emotional state.

Thought is a force even as electricity or gravitation. The human mind is a spark of the Almighty consciousness of God.

Whatever our powerful mind believes very intensely would instantly come to pass. The active expression of virtue give rise to the keenest intelligence.

What would you like to achieve by then?
_____
_____
_____

What do you want to be doing or not doing?
_____
_____
_____

How is your health? Who is around you?
_____
_____
_____

What is really exciting for you?
_____
_____
_____

AFFIRMATIVE JOURNALING

How could your life be the best it can be?

_____
_____
_____

What would you be really jazzed about?

_____
_____
_____

Imagine your future, six months from now, in as much detail as possible and write about it with an intensity of great feelings and emotions. Imagine it as whole heartedly as you can. Write about how you feel in the present tense as if it is already so at this moment.

_____
_____
_____
_____
_____
_____
_____
_____
_____
_____

The power of Affirmative Journaling lies in the act of writing, the act of affirming, and the act of pouring energy and redirecting your thoughts on what you want.

CHANGE YOUR BLUEPRINT THROUGH JOURNALING

Everything is possible!

BELIEVE!

FEEL!

Write as if it is already so!

Manifest!

TAKE ACTION!

Take more action!

Be still. Listen within!

All the answers you need are already there!

Write It Down!

Make It Happen!

Knowing What You Want and Getting It!

When you show your earnestness and intention by writing it down, something opens up. The word gets out, it creates a kind of Jungian synchronicity, a convergence of meaningful events. Write it down to be clear in communication to its possibility and then activity here will create related movements there. The universe wants to know your intentions so that you can be fully supported to manifest them and affirmative journaling will help you achieve that.

AFFIRMATIVE JOURNALING

We can energize our vision, manifest our life mission with every thought that we think and every word that we speak.

Affirmative writing opens up the entire world in your universe. It is a life changing event that occurs in the subconscious mind.

Every thought we think and every word we speak is an affirmation. Affirmation is something we all do, unconsciously or consciously. It is so powerful we do not even realize that we do it 24 hours a day, 7 days a week.

Everything we are now we have created into existence. All our self-talk, our internal dialogue, is a stream of affirmations. We affirm we are poor; we affirm we are rich, we affirm everybody love us; we affirm nobody loves us, we affirm we are awesome, magnificent and fantastic; we affirm we are failures, we have no money, we can't be rich, we affirm so many things about our lives, all that we say and think comes to pass. It is the power our subconscious thought brings forward into reality.

Perhaps you are saying that affirmations and being positive doesn't really work and that you have tried it. Maybe you even went to the store and bought yourself this amazing Blueprint journal with inspiring notes and a new blue ink pen. Now write your goals down and it will come to pass. I know, I know, in fact I really do know. I have tried those too.

I went to the store bought myself a brand new journal and colorful pens. I was ready to affirm! I wrote my affirmation down: I am a successful coach, I am a millionaire, but as my day progress for the rest of the day after I had finished with my journaling I kept on thinking, 'yeah, really me becoming successful, yeah right?' I was unconsciously affirming that I didn't have the tools or resources to become a millionaire or be a successful coach. Which affirmation do you think will win out? The negative one of course because it's part of a long standing, habitual way of looking at life, my Blueprint.

Some of us will say our affirmations once a day and complain for the rest of the day, this means that we are giving power to the negative affirmations because it is said with high intensity and with great feelings.

How do we practice affirming our purpose and changing our Blueprint beliefs? It is the positive repetition and energizing of a thought that brings about beliefs, creating opportunities for the thought or object of attraction to become a physical reality. We create things into form by our beliefs, positive or negative. Hopefully we are creating positive beliefs.

It takes zero faith. What it takes is imagination. If it's clear in your thought, it is even this moment barreling down on you like a Mack truck.

The minute we make an intention we create it instantaneously. It exists as an actual thing; however, we do not see it as yet because we are still operating from an old school limiting Blueprint belief. We are only aware of the reality we choose to observe. The physical manifestation remains enfolded outside of our current consciousness.

Don't give any time or intention or energy to the reality from which you are trying to escape. Tune in only to your intent. The

AFFIRMATIVE JOURNALING

simple reason we dial into programs we don't like is that we live in a world that worship limitations, such as negative news, gossip and hubris.

You know how sometimes we feel we are not really here, at least not in this moment and we have to drag ourselves back to the present, well this is where the magic happens. In that moment, step out of your comfort zone by repeatedly listening and acting on positive behaviors.

The now is the point of power, but we have named it difficult. The power to create with our thoughts is really easy. That's not even up for debate, but the stories we keep replaying in our mind, 'oh it is so difficult or yes I am working on it.' Try and notice for the next couple of minutes or for some of us perhaps the next couple of days how often you affirm that changing your thinking is difficult or challenging.

Pay attention to how often you say things have always been like that, or it runs in my family. We spend so much time affirming about what doesn't work that we miss the whole point, namely that we have the power to create something that does work.

If you know what you want, you can have it. Create what you want for yourself by believing in the infinite possibilities.

Put your heart on your Blueprint journal by knowing what you want and getting what you want by writing it down and making it happen.

Energize your thoughts by visualizing them as if it were real in your mind's eye. See yourself, happy, feeling accomplished, exuberant,

CHANGE YOUR BLUEPRINT THROUGH JOURNALING

content in the place where you want to be, doing what you love, being with the people you want to be with and giving what you have to give.

You can bring about anything by your thoughts. Align yourself with GOD Consciousness and you can bring any truth into material form. What you think, you create.

VI. ULTIMATE PURPOSE OF LIFE

"Do the one thing you think you cannot do. Fail at it. Try again. Do better the second time. The only people who never tumble are those who never mount the high wire. This is your moment. Own it."

— Oprah Winfrey

"You cannot solve a problem from the same consciousness that created it. You must learn to see the world anew."

— Albert Einstein

CHANGE YOUR BLUEPRINT THROUGH JOURNALING

What is your Ultimate purpose of life?

There may be a little voice in your head that keeps asking questions, such as:

> Is this it?
>
> Is this all there is to life?
>
> When do things get better?
>
> When do I get to really start living my life?

The answer to these questions is that life is meant to be filled with abundance and joy. Every day can be better than the one before. The way in which you start moving towards your best life is to begin by identifying what it is you truly want.

If everything worked out perfectly in your life, what would your life look like in one... five... ten years? How do you see yourself? How do you measure your success?

Such questions open us up to fresh new possibilities. To reflect on what matters most to us and what values might guide us through life.

Success isn't solely about reaching a financial or professional pinnacle. Success also involves cultivating solid relationships, striving to achieve health and well-being, giving back to others and generally leading a life of purpose. Success isn't an endpoint; it is a lifelong process.

ULTIMATE PURPOSE OF LIFE

As we progress in our own personal journey with our Blueprint journal, we want to constantly be on a path of self-awareness and introspection to rigorously examine our beliefs so that we can be as perfect of a mirror as possible to ourselves, reflecting back to our answers within.

"To realize our calling is our only real obligation and when you truly want something all the Universe conspires to make it happen."
—Rumi

What is your life's purpose?

We hide from the truth within. Our true potential is buried and forgotten by the gunk we have created for ourselves. It's scary to put your real self out there. It feels terrifying.

When we are growing up, generally we are not rewarded for being our true selves. So we learn how to adapt, how we 'should be' and end up putting on masks to hide ourselves.

The strategies we learn to hide at a young age are carried over into adulthood. Eventually these strategies we use to hide causes so much pain that we must change. Even though the reductionist worldview has been proved defective, it's still deeply ingrained and embedded into our Blueprint psyche. Neuroscientist tells us that 95 percent of our thoughts are controlled by our preprogrammed subconscious mind. Instead of actually believing and creating our life and our destiny we are conditioned to replay and relive the movie of the past.

However, most of us think we are running our lives with our brilliant ideas, we think we are creating our destiny by affirming our intentions, but in actuality we are simply recycling old tapes and automatic behaviors most of which we picked up before we were five years old. We are simply reacting to patterns we picked up before we had the intelligence to wisely choose. Most of the thoughts we assume are unquestioned beliefs we downloaded from others.

"We accept the language of the world and we forget the language of the soul."
— The Universe.

We buy everything else people believe about us. Usually we make their trash our truths. As a matter of fact, we need to remember that the universal truth for us is that we have gold sitting inside of us and it is our birth right to access our greatest potential and the real truth about us. We are AWESOME and we have unlimited potentialities.

We need to trust that we are not rediscovering our purpose, but we know our purpose and we are ready to live it out loud. A sense of happiness comes from when we feel fulfilled and that happens when we are fully living in the present.

What other people say about you, is their truth and not your truth. Don't give others your power by accepting their ideas and their beliefs. Listen with your heart and let your soul speak of who you are and what you have become by fulfilling your purpose and living in the now. This is your truth.

The main thing is to keep the main thing the main thing. Achieving your Ultimate purpose of life is to stay on purpose.

ULTIMATE PURPOSE OF LIFE

Discovering and living your purpose requires intuition, creativity and openness, as well as logic, will power and right action from moment to moment. In this process of Changing Your Blueprint Through Journaling we are opening up our creative mind and clearing our thoughts through daily consistent commitment.

Trust the power of your intuition and know that what you feel right at this moment is the right decision because your intuition is always on your side. Our intuition is really a sudden immersion of the soul into the universal current of life where we are able to know everything. Our heart knows how to interpret and therefore knows the right decision when our conscious mind is not able to decide on its own.

The moment you make a decision you have committed to an action of staying on purpose and to do the right thing and the Universe will conspire to make it happen. Be connected to the power within, it speaks to you, if you would give it an opportunity. Ask for guidance; pray for revelation as to the meaning of your intuitive mind. Choose to see everything that's happened as a pathway for growth, rather than a reason to stop.

Take life one day at a time. Don't future trip. Be present with what's happening now. Don't get caught in fear. Keep moving, remember, life is movement. Open up and ask for help. You aren't an island. You do have resources; all you have to do is look for them.

Identify your purpose in life and pursuing it serves as the only means by which you can live a satisfying life. In fact, the universe can only achieve perfection if all natural things continuously undergo a cycle of achieving their purpose, evolving into a higher

CHANGE YOUR BLUEPRINT THROUGH JOURNALING

being with a new ultimate purpose of life, and then pursuing that new goal. This concept, that we are in pursuit of, an ultimate purpose of life, exists within us all along.

Embrace and follow your ultimate purpose of life, know what it is that you always wanted to do and what makes you come alive when you are doing that. Fulfill your destiny in life by identifying your purpose and pursuing it.

Acknowledge your ultimate purpose of life. The language of the universe will attempt to reveal your ultimate purpose of life in many different ways, whether it be through mentors or signs. Whichever way you come to know your ultimate purpose of life it is important that you acknowledge it and take action to make your dreams become a reality. After all, when you really want something, the universe always conspires in your favor. It can be easy to realize your legend when you are young because at this point everything is clear and possible.

You are not afraid to dream and to yearn for what you'd like to see happen, but as time passes, a mysterious force begins to convince you that it will be impossible to realize your mission. Understand that you are able to pursue your ultimate purpose of life at any time because it is part of you.

You must always know what it is that you want. Create for yourself a goal in which you will be able to realize when you have accomplished it. Without a clear, explicit goal, it is impossible to ever achieve.

Sometime during your quest, you may feel as if the universe is not conspiring to help you achieve your purpose. It is said that the darkest hour of the night comes just before dawn. It's the simple

ULTIMATE PURPOSE OF LIFE

things in life that are the most extraordinary; only wise men are able to understand them.

Let Go of Your Fears and Doubts.

The main reason why the average person, will fail to seek out their Ultimate purpose of life, is safety. People are more concerned with making a name for themselves and being comfortable that they choose to settle for an average life.

People are always afraid of losing what they have, whether it's their life, or possessions and property. But this fear evaporates when we understand that our life stories and the history of the world were written by the same hand. By trusting in fate, you are able to free yourself from these fears. Don't give into your fears. If you do, you won't be able to follow your heart. There is only one thing that makes a dream impossible to achieve: the fear of failure. Without fearing failure, you are free to pursue your purpose.

Like the old saying "You cannot change the direction of the wind, you can only adjust your sails."

If you can concentrate always in the present, you'll be happy and fulfilled. The secret is here in the present. If you pay attention to the present you can improve upon it. And, if you improve on the present, what comes later will also be better. Each day, in itself, brings with it an eternity. Seize the day, and don't be distracted by the past, or future.

CHANGE YOUR BLUEPRINT THROUGH JOURNALING

When you really get to know your heart, you are able to listen to the soul of the universe.

Trust that you and your heart can always make the right decision. Once you have defined a goal, you should be able to realize when you have completed your ultimate purpose of life. Whatever you do, whether you are content where you are, or you strive for more, do not forget the lessons you have learned in your journey. After all, it is not necessarily the goal you must pursue, instead savor the time it takes you to get there.

VII. THE JOURNALING ROUTINE

First create what you want for yourself in your journal.

What happens to me is not as important as the meaning I assign to what happens to me. Journaling helps me sort through my experience and be intentional about my interpretation of my life.

In studying the lives of great people, one thing they have in common is journaling. If these incredible people thought it was important to keep a journal, then why not us?

Opportunity never stops knocking.

New friends are on their way.

The ideas you need will find you.

You'll have another chance.'

Things are getting brighter.

You are feeling lighter.

Love is rising. Be still. Prepare.

Others will call you lucky.

Your parents are so proud.

You ain't seen nothing yet.

Look out world a stirring.

A giant is waking up and that is you with your amazing journal.

CHANGE YOUR BLUEPRINT THROUGH JOURNALING

Journaling opens the door to the condition of many hearts.

As I said many famous writers have kept journals or diaries, for many, it is a creative necessity, for others, a place for exploration, and for some an art form in and of itself. For thirteen-year-old, Anne Frank her journal meant her life. "I want to be useful or bring enjoyment to all people, even those I've never met. I want to go on living even after my death! And that's why I'm so grateful to God for having given me this gift, which I can use to develop myself and to express all that's inside me!"
—Anne Frank, April 5, 1944

Anne Frank was insightful and mature. For a hostage, she was remarkably hopeful. I'm so glad that she wrote it all down, the curiosities, the fears, and the inundating declaration, "Despite everything, I believe that people are really good at heart." She did exactly what she set out to do, as expressed perfectly in the above quote. She has affected the lives of many people she never met, and she's still alive long after her tragic death. I'm sure her diary was the ultimate escape. She used it to travel far away from her immediate circumstances and to discover the uncharted territory of her burgeoning mind.

Not all of us will have the time to journal or to keep a record of our dailies. I think the more important part of journaling is to develop ourselves and express all that's in us. That should be our takeaway, the desire to develop and express ourselves.

Often times when I suggest people keep a journal some say, "I tried to keep a journal once and it didn't really work." I tried several times, too, before it worked. The way I made it work was I stopped getting upset at myself if I didn't write every day and I stopped expecting myself to write down the exact details of the day. Basically, I broke the journal-writing rules. I created for myself

THE JOURNALING ROUTINE

<u>Change Your Blueprint Through Journaling</u> template with consistent structure and as a result I was able to keep a journal, actually many journals.

I recommend that you practice journaling throughout your day starting in morning, afternoon and right before you say goodnight. Create a space in your life to bring about changes that will make you happier, start journaling in the beginning of your day, perhaps right after you get out of bed, or while you are having breakfast, or after you finished with some of your morning task(s), or maybe at your desk before you start your work or during a break or during lunch, basically anytime, just do it!

Start your day with the daily affirmation, affirming and creating the believe in your subconscious mind and practice repeating it for as many times as possible during your day, write it down so that you can see it in your mind's eye, keep affirming until it is embedded in your conditioned mind.

Write in your journal what would make your day great and create that type of atmosphere for the reality you want to have today. This bring you to the perfect opportunity to create the kindness that you want to bring forward in your life today by acknowledging the one act of kindness you can carry out during the course of this day.

Take a moment to reflect on what you are writing in your journal and carry that process out for an entire day.
Reflect on your notes at the end of the day; journaling then about the amazing things that happened during your day and what could have been done differently.

CHANGE YOUR BLUEPRINT THROUGH JOURNALING

You create your own reality and you do so because the thoughts that you are thinking cause you to emanate a vibrational frequency that the Law of Attraction is constantly responding to. And so, in all waking moments, you are creating your own points of attraction and everything that you experience is coming to you because of your vibrational emanation and the response of the Law of Attraction to that vibration. It is as if you are standing on a sort of spinning vibrational disc and only things of the same vibration can join you on your disc. Your disc changes depending upon the thoughts that you are thinking and the emotions that you are feeling.

My advice for you is to take a few minute before you start your day to create the journey of the most marvelous and fulfilling day in your life. Create the destiny you want by writing it down and setting the attention for it in your subconscious mind. Start out your day by a request to your subconscious mind.

VIII. DAILY AFFIRMATIONS

Affirmation for today:
I am deeply fulfilled by all that I do. I create for myself a powerful and successful day, today!

Start your day with beautiful and meaningful affirmations to inspire the beginning of the importance of creating a fascinating journey, daily.

The ten-minute period before you sleep and the ten-minute period after you awake is enormously influential on your subconscious mind. Only the most energizing and serene thoughts should be programmed into your mind at the beginning of your day.

An affirmation is a positive statement you say or think about yourself. Saying daily affirmations helps reprogram your negative self-talk so you can manifest more positive thinking, feeling and experiences. Use these powerful affirmations to enhance your life.

Keep in mind that it is the positive repetition and energizing of a thought that brings about belief, creating opportunities for the thought or object of attraction to become reality.

Every thought you think and every word you speak is an affirmation. All our self-talk, our mind babble is a stream of affirmations.

In this <u>Change Your Blueprint Through Journaling</u>, we start off with an affirmation. We want you to use these positive affirmations to prime your subconscious mind into forming beliefs consistently. You'll start to notice proof in your belief and begin to create evidence of that belief in your mind. Set the intention for the entire day by repeating the daily affirmation. Whenever you feel like you are going astray, gently bring your awareness back into affirmation mode.

The key is to be consistent with your daily affirmation. We need to teach the next generation of children from day one that they are responsible for their lives. Mankind greatest gift is that we have free choice. We can make our choices built from love or from fear. Man is made or unmade by himself.

"By the right choice he ascends. As a being of power, intelligence, and love, and the lord of his own thoughts, he holds the key to every situation."
—Allen

It's never too late to start a journey that satisfies your soul and strengthens your heart. It's worth it! We need to check in with ourselves and see how our thoughts come alive on paper, this is a meaningful and profound way to do it, that is, through Blueprint Journaling.

I strongly advise you to continually develop yourself and dare to bring forth all that is inside by affirming what you want in a powerful way with your thoughts and subconscious mind from moment to moment. The daily affirmation is a statement that defines how you want to be right now!

Every time you read an affirmation you prime your brain to start building this belief in your mind. With consistency, you will start to notice changes in your beliefs and begin to create confirmation of

DAILY AFFIRMATIONS

that affirmation in your mind. Do not underestimate the effectiveness of this exercise. If Jim Carrey, Will Smith, and Pam Grout found value in it, you can too!

When you choose to write an affirmation, you are making a conscious decision to heal your life and move forward on the path of positive change and the time for that positive change is now! There is no time like the present for you to take control of your thoughts.

Keeping up with your affirmations is not hard work. It can be an exuberant experience as you lift the burden of old negative beliefs and release them to the nothingness from whence they came.

Words affect the mind in a pronounced way. Whether they are spoken or written they are powerful influences. While what you say to others is important, even more important is what you say to yourself.

You are what you think about all day long. You are also what you say to yourself all day long. If you say that you are old and tired, this negative affirmation will be manifested in your external reality.

If you say you are weak and lack enthusiasm, this too will be the nature of your world. But if you say that you are healthy, dynamic and fully alive, your life can be transformed.

CHANGE YOUR BLUEPRINT THROUGH JOURNALING

You see, the words you say to yourself affect your self-image and your self-image determines what actions you take. For example, if your self-image is one of a person who lacks the confidence to do anything of value, you will only be able to take actions which are aligned with this trait. On the other hand, if your self-image is one of a radiant individual who is fearless, again, all your actions will correspond to this quality.

Your self-image is a self-fulfilling prophecy of sorts.

IX. PRACTICE BEING THANKFUL

<u>Daily by writing it down and connecting from within.</u>

<u>I am Thankful for... Finishing my book.</u>

<u>I am Thankful for the difficult decision I had to make.</u>

<u>I am ever Thankful for the rain.</u>

<u>I am Thankful for everything working out in my life.</u>

<u>Thank you!!!</u>

Be thankful for everything, for everything in our life has a reason. I am because we are, it is all about love and how we are all connected. One of our greatest gifts in this life is having the ability to choose what we focus on regardless of what is happening on the outside. However, if we are calm and still on the inside, we can then accomplish anything we set out to. Calmness is the doorway to clarity. The best way we can start out our day is to be thankful. Look around, what's not to be thankful for? I can't imagine anything not to be thankful for in my life.

When you express being thankful, you raise the vibrations around you to a higher frequency. You create positive energy that emanates out from you and returns to you as wonderful experiences. You become magnetic.

CHANGE YOUR BLUEPRINT THROUGH JOURNALING

Good things and good people gravitate towards you because you're such a joy and delight to be around. An attitude of being so thankful is naturally attractive. It has the power to turn challenges into possibilities, problems into solutions and losses into gains. It shifts the energy, expands our vision and allows us to see what might normally be invisible to someone with a limiting approach.

Being Thankful is a prayer for goodness to abound. I believe that the words 'thank you' are two of the most beautiful words we can declare. They can light up someone's face and help the other person know that he or she is appreciated. It opens the doors to our heart and allows us to feel connected. Let us spend as many moments as we can every day by being thankful for all the good that's in our lives.

Affirm: I express gratitude and thanksgiving every day, in every way. Doing so is an important part of my life.

Before we go to sleep we should say out loud the things that we are grateful for, all the significant, insignificant, extraordinary, ordinary stuff of our life. It is such a small and humble practice and yet, if we do this we will be amazed of how we sleep better, holding what lightens and softens our life ever so briefly at the end of the day.

Every moment, every happiness, every sadness, every kindheartedness, every sad moment, every unfulfilled desire, every moment of togetherness, moments of loneliness, families, friends, life, death, moments of insecurity all these things are in our life for reason known or unknown. Why we had to go through such moments we have no control over? Why our decision seems wrong

PRACTICE BEING THANKFUL

at the moment? Why we had to suffer? Why we lost our family or why have we separated?

Our life so fast and ever changing. We go through this process in our life for a very distinctive reason. Changes had to occur for our soul evolution, our life mission, and our duty in fulfilling our personal calling. So be thankful for all of it. Being Thankful is a great way to keep yourself in a positive state of mind.

"If the only prayer you say in your life is 'thank you,' that would suffice."
—Meister Eckhart

Being Thankful means having gratitude, counting your blessings, noticing simple pleasures and acknowledging everything that you receive. It means learning to live your life as if everything were a miracle and being aware on a continuous basis of how much you've been given.

Gratitude shifts your focus from what your life lacks to the abundance that is already present. In addition, studies have shown the surprising life improvements that can stem from the practice of being thankful.

Being Thankful makes us happier and more resilient, it strengthens relationships, it improves health and it reduces stress in our life. Are you ready to become Thankful for everything in your life?

At times our own light goes out and is rekindled by a spark from another person. Each of us have a cause to think with deep gratitude of those who have lighted the flame within us and for that we are usually ever grateful.

CHANGE YOUR BLUEPRINT THROUGH JOURNALING

We should give up trying to pay back the people in this world who has sustained our lives. In the end, maybe it is wiser to surrender before the miraculous scope of human generosity and to continue saying thank you with honest feelings and sincerity.

The experience of being thankful is counting one's blessings. It is the feeling that embodies the word 'Thank you.' It is the unexpected reward of a kind deed that is magically produced by our brain. It is the cute, tingly feeling in your body that makes you smile at strangers.

Thank you for being a part of my journey!!!

X. VISUALIZING YOUR PERFECT DAY

What would make today great?

Smile with everyone I come into contact with, regardless of the situation.

Practice stream of consciousness journaling.

Take extra time for myself.

Work on my project.

Sleep before 9PM.

"Every new day is another chance to change your life"
—Unknown

CHANGE YOUR BLUEPRINT THROUGH JOURNALING

Every day we get to choose our attitude. Today I declare that I can and I am choosing to be positive! The fundamental principle to keep in mind is the importance of starting your day off well. As I've suggested the thoughts you think and the actions you take in the first ten minutes after you awake have a marked impact on the rest of your day.

Take a moment and start to focus on here and now. This is difficult for everyone, it can be very difficult to focus on what is directly in front of you and ensure that you are fully present by creating what it is you want for your day.

Before you get out of bed close your eyes and imagine your perfect day with great clarity. This is a way to hone in on what you're really after in your personal and professional life. Remember that in order to set the intention for your picture-perfect day you need to know what your ideal day looks like, what it smells like, tastes like, feels like and most important what you want to create for our self today. Nothing has meaning except for the meaning you bring to it.

There's a reason why the saying "When life throws you lemons, make lemonade" has been around for years. When things aren't going right, ask yourself, 'Could things be worse?' or 'Is there anything I can learn from this that can be beneficial to me?'

Create a Blueprint journal record of your ideal day so that you can manifest your day's achievement. When you look at what this day includes, also try and look at what it doesn't include, like dealing with difficult moments, or trying to do a million things at once and getting frustrated by not anticipating that you have the strength and the will power to change and deal with any situation in a different way.

VISUALIZING YOUR PERFECT DAY

Have the courage to take action to explore, to believe in yourself, to own your own choices by creating what you desire.

What we focus on expands.

Now, imagine your day, your perfect day; getting up, going to work, whatever it is you have to do.

How do you envision your day as you walk, stretch, get dressed...?

Will you listen to some uplifting music?

Will you watch the sun come up or perhaps go for a quick walk in natural surroundings if you feel up to it?

What will be the first thing you do? The second?

What will you eat?

How will you'd spend your time?

Ultimately what will you create for yourself?

What you don't want to do is equally as important as what you do want to do. Take steps to eliminate those things from your life or at the very least, to reframe your thoughts and create a new process by paying attention to your visualization process.

What things immediately pop out at you?

How you can work out with the things you want to do and that would make today great.

CHANGE YOUR BLUEPRINT THROUGH JOURNALING

Laugh whether you feel like it or not. Laughing is medicine for the soul. Even if you don't feel like it, look in the mirror and laugh for a couple of minutes. You can't help but feel fantastic. Visualize your ideal day, in clear details. Sit with the thought, breathe it in, dream about it, write it down, talk it out, paint it...

Honor the past, learn from it, accept it and let it go. Don't obsess or worry about the future. Life is more manageable when you are grounded in the present. More often than not, there is a positive aspect to things that happen, even those that feel negative. Try to view it in a different light and you may find your attitude turn around.

Life is beautiful even when you think you can't take another step. Change your consciousness towards the things that bothers you and create for yourself a most perfect day.

XI. BE KIND WHENEVER POSSIBLE

"Thanksgiving and praise open in your consciousness the way for spiritual growth and supply to come to you."

—Paramahansa Yogananda

"Kindness is a language which the deaf can hear and the blind can see."

—Mark Twain

CHANGE YOUR BLUEPRINT THROUGH JOURNALING

What is Kindness?

Kindness is a behavior marked by ethical characteristics, a pleasant disposition, and a concern for others. It is known as a virtue, and recognized as a value in many cultures and religions.

<u>What is one act of kindness I can do today?</u>

<u>I give up complaining for an entire day, Woohoo!!!</u>

<u>I surprise my friend with flowers.</u>

<u>I spend 15 minutes in silence.</u>

When you express kindness, you raise the vibrations around you to a higher frequency. You create positive energy that emanates out from you and returns to you as wonderful experiences. Kindness is a prayer for goodness to overflow.

<u>You become magnetic.</u>
Give a prayer of thanks for all you have.
Work on your gratitude list.

Why Kindness? We all struggle. We all stress. Nevertheless, we also all love. In reality, we can't help but love! It's part of the conditioned mind. You can't have 'humankind' without kind, after all.

The problem is that, when we get wrapped up in our own problems, we forget to take care of others because our brains go into self-preservation mode. Don't get me wrong, taking care of yourself is super important we can't take care of others without taking care

BE KIND WHENEVER POSSIBLE

of ourselves. We just need to remember to look beyond us and see the need in others as well as ourselves. It can sometimes be hard, but it is instantaneously, demonstrably worthwhile because it only takes one kind act to strongly affect us. You know the sort of kindness we're talking about. It's the person who is enthusiastically praising their co-worker's hard work, or a stranger covering a bill for a struggling parent, or the carpenter dressing up as a superhero at the hospital. These are the little moments that have a huge impact and stays with us forever. These are the things that connect us back to our humanity. This should remind us of how much love there is in the world and we should feel so good that these kindnesses inspire us to keep on spreading kindness.

We know how important kindness is. Scientific studies have shown that random acts of kindness are good for us! Kindness improves your life satisfaction by increasing your sense of belonging and self-worth and kindness improves your health by decreasing anxiety, depression and blood pressure. Here is the best part, these benefits apply to the giver of kindness, the recipient of kindness and anyone who witnesses kindness! Every kindness improves the lives of at least three people.

So, why kindness?
Scientifically? Because it's good for our health.
Economically? Because it's free.
Practically? Because it's easy.
Socially? Because it improves the world.
But what is the real reason, of course it is that one act kindness is the key to lasting happiness.

We should practice at least one random deed of kindness every day. This can be to a stranger or for a loved one and can be whatever we choose. The rippling effect starts with one. Just one

CHANGE YOUR BLUEPRINT THROUGH JOURNALING

person to hold open a door. One person to leave a note on someone's car, complimenting their awesome parking skills. One person to write a thank you note to a teacher. One person to be a spark of kindness when another really needs it. Husband to show his wife appreciation with some flowers.

Any kindness will put a smile on the face of another, it will show your love for your fellow man and brings inner happiness to your soul. This will help in making this sometimes difficult life a more fulfilled one.

Remember no kindness is ever wasted.

What stops and prevent us from being kind?

Do we think too much and feel too little?

I firmly believe that we need less technology, what we need more is humanity. More than expertise, we need kindness and togetherness. At times our own light goes out and is rekindled by a spark from another person. Each of us have a cause to think with deep gratitude of those who have lit the flame within us. Who is that someone whom made a difference in your life? It's easy to think of kindness as an innate talent, something you either possess or don't. But that's not the case. Kindness is a skill and like any skill, it can be developed with practice and repetition, until you have become a master at it. Practicing this for over ten thousand hours!

"Kindness unlocks the fullness of life. It turns what we have into enough, and more. It turns denial into acceptance, chaos to order,

BE KIND WHENEVER POSSIBLE

confusion to clarity. It can turn a meal into a feast, a house into a home, a stranger into a friend."
—Melody Beattie

Now it is your chance to do the same. Be kind, smile at anyone you meet, and acknowledge everyone who is working, from the person who takes your money at the cash register at the local gas station or store, the guard at the drop off zone at your school who watches your kid(s), the garbage man/woman who picks up your trash, the cop who works at night to keep you safe, the fireman who stops to get a sandwich because they just got back from a fire and don't have time to sit down to a meal. In short, anyone ... be kind to them... for without any of them, our society and hence our life would not function properly and it costs you nothing to make someone's day brighter simply by being kind to them. We need to spend as many moments as we can to be grateful for all the good that's in our lives. There is something called the collective agreement it is how we all get along. So make someone's day, thank them for doing what they do!

One of the best ways to increase our own happiness is to do things that make other people happy. In countless studies, kindness and generosity have been linked to greater life satisfaction, stronger relationships and better mental and physical health. Generous people even live longer. Leading research indicates that we can address ever-increasing imbalances in our society by changing the way we view and interact with the world. We each are part of a whole and everything we do, every thought, word and deed affects the whole. Happiness is not something ready-made, it comes from our actions. If we keep our eyes open, we are going to discover that kindness is all around us.

CHANGE YOUR BLUEPRINT THROUGH JOURNALING

Kind behavior comes naturally when we're feeling a sense of compassion and connection with others. Everything we think, say, and do matters, and we have a free willpower to be to be kind, moment to moment it affects how we feel. As a firm believer in kindness, I am always looking for ways to teach myself the profound power of kind thoughts toward life, kind words towards others and kind actions towards family, friends, classmates and strangers. Kindness also has an amazing win-win affect, because you think you are doing good for others, but you end up benefiting in the process!

I believe that the best way to realize our full potential is to raise our collective consciousness by embracing that we are all connected and that kindness toward ourselves, others, animals, the planet and all living thing is the path to peace and happiness and for this awareness to guide all of our decisions and ways we interact with one another.

Practice keeping track of the kindness in your life by journaling one act of kindness through your Blueprint journaling and increasing the habit of making this a daily repetition. Too often we underestimate the power of a touch, a smile, a kind word, a listening ear, an honest compliment, or the smallest act of caring, all of which have the potential to turn our life around.

Visualize the ways you have been kind to people and how they have been kind to you. Writing about the kindness that you can do today and staying on purpose with it, by being systematic, will help you think in a more positive way.

You'll be surprised how much easier it is to be kind, when you make an effort to think about kindness all the time!

BE KIND WHENEVER POSSIBLE

We want to be committed to doing one kind act for someone different every day for an entire year!

Life is short, break the rules.

Forgive quickly, kiss slowly, love truly, laugh uncontrollably and

never regret anything that makes you smile and brings joy to others.

Imagine a world.

Where people look out for each other.

Where we all pay it forward.

Where success is measured in selfless acts.

Where kindness is the philosophy of life.

"LOVE THYSELF LAST"

Love thyself last. Look near, behold thy duty
To those who walk beside thee down life's road.
Make glad their days by little acts of beauty
And help them bear the burden of earth's load.

Love thyself last. Look far and find the stranger,
Who staggers 'neath his sin and his despair;
Go lend a hand, and lead him out of danger,

CHANGE YOUR BLUEPRINT THROUGH JOURNALING

To heights where he may see the world is fair.

Love thyself last. The vastnesses above thee
Are filled with Spirit Forces, strong and pure
And fervently, these faithful friends shall love thee:
Keep thou thy watch o'er others and endure.

Love thyself last; and oh, such joy shall thrill thee,
As never yet to selfish souls was given.
Whate'er thy lot, a perfect peace will fill thee,
And earth shall seem the ante-room of Heaven.

Love thyself last, and thou shall grow in spirit
To see, to hear, to know, and understand.
The message of the stars, lo, thou shall hear it,
And all God's joys shall be at thy command.
—Ella Wheeler Wilcox

XII. STAYING ON TRACK WITH YOUR PURPOSE

Awesome things that happened today...

<u>I finished my project.</u>

Choose to be grateful for the day.
Choose to look on the bright side.
Choose to focus on the possibilities.
Choose to be amazed by all of it.

"Look to this day:
For it is life, the very life of life.
In its brief course
Lie all the varieties and realities of your existence.
The bliss of growth,
The glory of action,
The splendor of achievement
Are but experiences of time.
For yesterday is but a dream
And tomorrow is only a vision;
And today well-lived, makes
Yesterday a dream of happiness
And every tomorrow a vision of hope.
Look well therefore to this day;
Such is the salutation to the ever-new dawn!"

— Kalidasa

CHANGE YOUR BLUEPRINT THROUGH JOURNALING

Create a few moments in your day where you share the positive things, big or small, to celebrate you!

We need to acknowledge at least once a day the amazing things that is happening in our life. We need to see the difficult things that worked out in our situations and circumstances in our physical space. Make a habit of this act daily to truly expand your heart to acknowledge the inspiring moments of all that happen in the course of your day. Think about it, feel good about it, enjoy the moment, be thankful for the experience and write it down.

Celebrating your wins is acknowledging your journey to your personal accomplishment, progress, thoughts patterns and your true potential.

Your awesomeness is your personal collection of the expected and unexpected abundance of truly miraculous things that you experience in your day.

No exceptions, stop complaining!
Stop sharing bad news, just practice sharing the best things that happen to you today.

This will have such a positive impact on the rest of your day, or evening with family, friends, your studies or you name it. When you write about the awesome things, you are counting your blessing in the day. This has the effect of allowing you to prime your brain in reverse and can change not just relationships with your love ones, it can change your relationship with yourself. You will feel fascinated to look at what you have accomplished.

STAYING ON TRACK WITH YOUR PURPOSE

There is no limitation to how you can feel about your success!!! We need to write to express our journey of accomplishment and a note to our higher self so that we can feel empowered by our own voice and potential within.

This is a way of connecting to elements which offers significant value to your life. The more you build your awareness of your accomplishments the more you will have to celebrate. Focus on all your wins and select a few to celebrate each day.

It is CRITICAL to take a moment to STOP and CELEBRATE what you have already succeeded in. It's easy to recognize areas in your life that could be improved, but people often overlook the pieces of their lives they can currently be proud of.

While it is important to set goals with the aim of bettering yourself, it is equally important to celebrate the things in your life in which you have already successfully completed. Instead of getting perpetually bogged down trying to achieve the bigger goal, it's a good idea to give your self-confidence a boost by acknowledging the baby steps that you have accomplished today.

Small wins are progress posts on the way to your goal. I believe it is the little things and maybe it is when we think of a goal our mind usually gravitates toward the dramatic transformation. We need to understand that all positive changes are constructive. I believe in the possibilities of change. As the saying goes, "Rome was not built in a day."

Too many of us are worried about change and taking another step forward. We focus on the large expanse between where we are now and where we want to be. That's exactly where we shouldn't

CHANGE YOUR BLUEPRINT THROUGH JOURNALING

be placing our attention. Success isn't built by daily yearning for a distant goal; it's in creating and celebrating the small wins we accomplish along the way. Pat yourself on the back you have come 'a far way's today and you are doing remarkably well!

Never ever minimize the importance of celebrating small wins at the end of your day. It is more important than you think. You may believe it is too costly or time-consuming to get yourself together, to sit and be with yourself to celebrate, but rest assured, it might prove even more costly if you don't take the time to celebrate the beauty of your day. You have to understand how important recognition is.

Acknowledge the small wins, not just the big wins. Record the small wins so you can feel a sense of success. Big wins can be relatively rare. If, however, we acknowledge the smaller wins, we can boost our mental health and mood and that of our entire environment. This is because we are making progress in meaningful ways. Show visible progress toward the long-term goals. Research shows that when people can see visible progress and experience small wins along the way, they become more engaged, productive and creative in their life.

Share the celebration of your wins, a cheering culture, is usually a blessing. When you involve your friends and family in your wins to celebrate the success of something you have accomplished, then everyone gets to share in your success and feel a part of the win. This is powerful! Cheering is unifying, it creates an atmosphere of fellowship and a willingness to accept each other and buoy one another. It acknowledges success. Celebrate each other wins, we need to feel a sense of achievement and joy and hold the same vision for others as they celebrate their wins.

STAYING ON TRACK WITH YOUR PURPOSE

Hold the Vision of success for yourself daily and you will begin to feel powerful and have a sense of peace and joy in your life! Don't be afraid to celebrate how far you have come. You would be shocked at how many people just check off their daily accomplishments and never realize that in order to feel the power of success they must celebrate the small steps.

Take a moment to be proud of yourself. Go out for ice cream. Make a big deal about it. Feel happy and allow friends and family to compliment you and tell you that they are proud of you.

Let yourself enjoy that moment because that is what all of this is for. It is about showing yourself and agreeing with the universe that you are capable of success. If you can't take a step back and celebrate, you are going to have a difficult time moving ahead and believing in your true self.

Now!

Go!

Stake your claim!

Hold out your hands.

Move, get ready, give thanks.

Imagine, and let go.

Act, and have faith. Persist.

CHANGE YOUR BLUEPRINT THROUGH JOURNALING

Do what you can, when you can, all you can because never again, not in a million years, not over ten thousand lifetimes, will you ever again be as close as you are today!

"Live life as if everything is rigged in your favor."
—Rumi

XIII. YOUR THOUGHTS & IDEAS

What have I done differently today?

"The ultimate measure of a man is not where he stands in moments of comfort and convenience, but where he stands at times of challenge and controversy."

—Mark Twains

"I believe that the best way to inspire others to change, is to be the change you wish to see."

—Mahatma Gandhi

CHANGE YOUR BLUEPRINT THROUGH JOURNALING

In order to have the maximum benefit and transformation with these journaling questions, it is essential to create a sacred space within our mind, body and soul.

>Since our programming leads to our thoughts;
>And our thoughts lead to our feelings;
>Our feelings lead to our actions;
>Our actions lead to our results.

We need to change our Blueprint programming, to take the first essential step to changing our results by doing things differently.

This will allow you to get a good look at those signs that remind you where you are going, to let you know when you are on track, and to fully experience the journey. As I have said before, we think we're running our lives with our brilliant ideas and thoughts. We think we're affirming our intentions and creating new possibilities, but in reality we're simply recycling old tapes, knee jerk conditioning, and automatic behaviors, most of which we picked up before we were five.

"Man's chief delusion is his conviction that there are causes other than his own state of consciousness."
—Neville Goddard

You don't need an overhaul to improve the quality of your life. Just a few steps can help to boost your well-being and make your days more meaningful. The great part is that you can start today with your Blueprint Journal by listing the things you can do differently or have done differently today. Empower yourself to change what you can, and let go of the rest. Don't expend your energy trying to control others. Focus on yourself and the things you can do differently.

We all have a reason deep inside of us that motivates every

YOUR THOUGHTS & IDEAS

decision that we make and every action that we take. You are here and you want to go there; you dreamed-of life and because both are physical places, it would seem that you must manipulate the physical world to go from here to there Aha! This is the ultimate illusion.

Physical places are simply mirages, reflections of an inner world, the world of your thoughts. So to get from here to there, you must do your manipulating within and use your thoughts and creativity to lead the way. Recognize a thought worth dwelling on, and create from that thought your idea to accomplish your mission.

The greatest thing about being human is the ability to take charge of our lives. Accept accountability today. Realize that, though your subconscious beliefs steer your life, you control those beliefs. Use <u>Change Your Blueprint Through Journaling</u> as the platform to burst free of your cocoon, realize your true inner power, take control of your life and accept the amazing person you are!

Take control of your life today!

Make the choice, Change Your Blueprint and Change your Life!

Take a moment and focus on the here and now, what you did or are willing to do differently. Stop and see what it is that's keeping you stuck right now. Often times it's a blind spot, so taking time to mull things over helps you see clearly. Is it a decision you're afraid to make? Are certain people bringing you down? Are you in a cycle of negative thinking? Look around you to how this blind spot is affecting your life. Is it only at home, at school or at work? And finally listen to what your heart and mind tells you about what you

CHANGE YOUR BLUEPRINT THROUGH JOURNALING

need to do. Learning to reflect on your inner thoughts and feelings will help you put them into action.

Positive visualization increases the likelihood of success. We largely create our own realities through our thoughts and intentions. So clarify your thoughts by writing them out in your journal.

For life improvement, I suggest you put life on pause, for at least a few moments a day, and consider what you'd like to accomplish today, and the vibe you want to carry on with in a whole new sense. It can be difficult to change and to do things that are Blueprinted in our conditioned mind and to train yourself to think differently, but this change is so rewarding when the effort is made. So begin changing the things that you want by making that mental shift. Start small if you have to, but start today. Focus on the things you can change instead of what you cannot. Change one tiny part of your life and you change your energy about the very part of your life you were stressed out about.

Insanity: doing the same thing over and over again and expecting different results.
—Albert Einstein

XIV. KEEP YOUR VISION IN FRONT OF YOU

"Life is one big road with lots of signs. So when you riding through the ruts, don't complicate your mind. Flee from hate, mischief and jealousy. Don't bury your thoughts, put your vision to reality. Wake Up and Live!"

—Bob Marley

"Vision is the art of seeing what is invisible to others."

—Jonathan Swift

CHANGE YOUR BLUEPRINT THROUGH JOURNALING

It may look like the difficulties is going to defeat you. But you need to keep telling yourself that no difficult moment can shorten one second of your divine destiny. You are keeping your purpose in front of you by writing it down and making it happen a lot more.

The first step in your goal is to write it down, keeping your vision in front of you is about knowing what you want and making it happen.

On the way to your destiny, there will be times of testing where you don't see anything happening. But you've got to stay on purpose and keep on moving towards the direction of your vision.

I kept hearing, seeing and reading about all these celebrity stories, during the process of creating this Blueprint journal. These stories kept popping up, like a constant reminder towards my goal, this Blueprint journal. They were so present that I couldn't help but smile each time it would appear in an article or in a story line which made me grateful to the universe for conspiring in my favor, just so that I stayed on purpose.

In the early 1980s Jim Carrey walked up the hills of Hollywood and wrote himself a check for ten million dollars. On the memo line he wrote, "For service rendered." For years the comedian carried the check around him, long before he was paid that kind of money. Now he is one of the highest paid entertainers in the industry, getting twenty million dollars for a film.

Scott Adams, creator of the comic Dilbert, has a whole string of writing down his dreams and making it a reality for himself. It all came true one step at a time. I think this is how he puts it. "When you write down a goal, you observe things happening that will make

KEEP YOUR VISION IN FRONT OF YOU

that objective more likely to materialize." As a technology worker in a cubicle, Adams kept on staring up at the ceiling doodling off his office desk. Then he began to write, fifteen times a day I will become a syndicated cartoonist." Through dedication and commitment to making this his reality he was rejected many times, but he persevered and then it happened. He signed a contract for his comic strip to be syndicated. And just then he started writing "I will be the best cartoonist on the planet." Well what to say about all of his vision and what his purpose is? Dilbert is syndicated in almost 2,000 newspapers worldwide. The Dilbert zone website gets over 100,000 visitors a day. Now Adams write fifteen times a day I will win a Pulitzer Prize!

Suze Orman, Author of the number one New York Times Bestseller, <u>The 9 Steps to Financial Freedom</u>, shared how she started out in her journey to success. She got herself a job at Merrill Lynch and was terrified that she would not be able to meet her sales quota. The most she had made up until then was four hundred dollars a month as a waitress.

"I created what I wanted for myself, first in my journal. Every day I'd write in my journal over and over again, I am young, powerful and successful, earning at least $10,000 a month." Even after she had surpassed that figure she kept on journaling about how successful she was and continues to be. What she did was, she replaced the fear and her belief of inadequacy, with a message of endless possibility.

Research have shown that we move towards what we consistently see. Keep this journal with you as a symbol to remind you of your purpose and to create the type of day you want in your life. When you see some of your writing long enough it gets into your

CHANGE YOUR BLUEPRINT THROUGH JOURNALING

subconscious mind, it eventually touches your soul and that's when you know it is happening in real time.

What we keep in front of us becomes our affirmation, it creates a space of our imagination to be our reality.

Recognizing that our words have creative power is a key ingredient to our success. Whenever we speak, something, either good or bad, we give life to what we are saying. Often time we say too many negative things about our lives, our future, our family, our relationship, job, bank accounts etc. What we fail to realize is that we limit our lives by our words and thoughts.

"With the fruit of a man's mouth his stomach will be satisfied; He will be satisfied with the product of his lips. Death and life are in the power of the tongue, and those who love it will eat its fruit."
—Proverb 18:21

This means we will get exactly what we are creating with our words.

What is your vision? With no vision we can get stuck and live a life without purpose. As I am reinforcing, create your life by being systematic for an entire year. Stay the course!

"It matters not how strait the gate,
How charged with punishments the scroll,
I am the master of my fate:
I am the captain of my soul."
—Invictus

XV. ASK! CREATE! MANIFEST!

"By choosing your thoughts,
and by selecting which emotional currents you will release
and which you will reinforce,
you determine the quality of your Light.
You determine the effects that you will have upon others,
and the nature of the
experiences of your life."

—Gary Zukav

"Manifest plainness,
embrace simplicity,
reduce selfishness,
have few desires."

—Lao Tzu

CHANGE YOUR BLUEPRINT THROUGH JOURNALING

Everything you are, everything your life is, and everything you have, you have created.

Give yourself a tap on the back! All the wonder and beauty, all the experiences you have drawn to your life and what you have become as a result, you have chosen. Remember we create our lives, either consciously, or unconsciously.

Since we create our life intentionally or unintentionally, why not go all out and design the most magnificent life of our dreams?

Dream BIG!

Be wacky!   *Get good crazy!*

USE YOUR IMAGINATION!

Write what you want your life to be. What you want to be! Give yourself a chance; you will be surprised what your heart can see in store for you. Begin by writing in your Blueprint journal that was created just as perfect as you are.

Look at what you are and what you have already created in your life. See all the beauty that exists from moment to moment. If there is anything you do not want, change it! Just as you created it, you can create something else in its place. So choose what you want, and replace those old crusty fears and limiting wants with fresh budding beliefs and abundance. Anything you want... Go right ahead and order it!

Abundant life is our birthright.

ASK! CREATE! MANIFEST!

This universe is ours.
Just as God created universes upon universes through His infinite imagination, so can we!
He created us and all the abilities He has, we have.

When we still feel guilty for asking what we want, we are like a starving king who sitting at his royal banquet, that is, overflowing with every delicacy possible asks merely for a raisin.

Every moment of your life your good is seeking you out! All things you need for your progress are moving towards you. Trust and know with certainty that all your wants are waiting for you. If you do not use it or take it, it is still there waiting for you. Have no doubts about it! Whatever you can see and believe, is already yours! See it, feel it, and make it happen!

What are you waiting for? **ASK! CREATE! MANIFEST!**

Our deepest fear is not that we are inadequate. Our deepest fear is that we are powerful beyond measure. It is our light, not our darkness that most frightens us.

We ask ourselves, who am I to be brilliant, gorgeous, talented, and fabulous? Actually, who are you not to be? You are a child of God. You playing small does not serve the world. And as we let our own light shine, we unconsciously give other people permission to do the same. As we are liberated from our own fear, our presence automatically liberates others.

Who we have become as a result of the life that we have lived and the experiences we have had, is what we bring to the present moment. We're always in the mode of practice, of mastery, until we are Self-Realized.

CHANGE YOUR BLUEPRINT THROUGH JOURNALING

The first order before you take action in this journal is to clear your mind. Without clarity, it is hard to see where you are going, and what you must do next. When we clear our mind, we can access our intuition that is right there beneath the surface waiting to guide you in your life.

There's an invisible energy force that is constantly available for our use, and we haven't bothered to turn it on. We think of life as a random crapshoot, c'est la vie.

It is hard to build a building without a plan, so it is hard to make your desires a reality when you do not have an idea of what you want. Makes sense, right? So how do we create miraculous things in our lives, even when we do not know what we want? How do we stay on purpose with our lives, without having a Master Plan?

Can you imagine how wonderful it would be if you could live your life without ever being criticized by anyone? Wouldn't it be wonderful to feel totally at ease, totally comfortable? You would get up in the morning, and you would know you were going to have a wonderful day, because everybody would love you and nobody would criticize you or put you down. You'd just feel great.

You know what? You can give this to yourself. You can make the experience of living with you the most wonderful experience imaginable. You can wake up in the morning so thrilled to find yourself and feel the joy of spending another day with you.

Remember, every time you make a judgment or a criticism, you are sending something out that is going to come back to you.

ASK! CREATE! MANIFEST!

Let's affirm:

I notice all the good experiences coming my way today.

I express infinite love and gratitude.

I lovingly speak up for myself.

I attract respect.

I am constantly creating more good in my life.

Everything falls into place today.

All is well!

CHANGE YOUR BLUEPRINT THROUGH JOURNALING

I am surrounded by only positive, kind, loving and wise people in my personal, professional, relationship and spiritual life. I am unconditionally loved by divine Power and people around me. I am attracting positive circumstances, abundance, happiness and prosperity in my life. I love myself and people around me. I am spiritually aligned with the infinite universe and I am safe. All is well.

I believe we create our own lives. And we create it by our thinking, feeling patterns in our belief system. I think we're all born with this huge canvas in front of us and the paintbrushes and the paint and we choose what to put on this canvas.

"Your body is the harp of your soul and it is yours to bring forth sweet music from it or confused sounds."
— Kahlil Gibran

XVI. CHANGE YOUR BLUEPRINT JOURNALING!

"Listen, dear journal, I will tell you what I will tell no one else."

—Ella Gertrude Clanton

"Keep a notebook. Travel with it, eat with it, sleep with it. Slap into it every stray thought that flutters up into your brain. Cheap paper is less perishable than gray matter. And lead pencil markings endure longer than memory."

—Jack London

"I don't want to live in a hand-me-down world of others' experiences. I want to write about me, my discoveries, my fears, my feelings, about me."

—Helen Keller

CHANGE YOUR BLUEPRINT THROUGH JOURNALING

I believe in living a life that is constantly moving forward, a life that is flexible, dynamic and fluid. I believe past errors and failures are valuable lessons for growth and progress. Even so, there are life-lessons where the price is too high, where the lessons could and should have been learned another way.

Change Your Blueprint to New Patterns. We all have things we'd like to change about ourselves. Even those who are honestly happy with themselves will usually admit to areas where they'd like to improve or grow. Besides, life is all about growth. If you're not growing you're moving backward. It's like your reading habits. If you practice reading every day, your mind will grow and get a better understanding of what you are reading. But if you don't practice reading your mind will atrophy and the same with journaling.

You can't stand still in life because we aren't static beings. But where do you start? How do you choose what to change about yourself? How do you decide what your new Blueprint will be? The best time to start was 15 years ago, the second best time is now! That may sound tiresome, but how many opportunities have you let pass by because you failed to act on them? Do not brood over lost opportunities, instead grasp them with both hands.

Success is hastened or delayed by one's habits. It's not your passing inspirations or brilliant ideas so much as your everyday mental habits that control your life. Habits of thought are Blueprinted magnets that draw to you, certain things, people, and conditions. Good habits of thought enable you to attract benefits and opportunities. Bad habits of thought attract you to materially minded persons and to unfavorable environments. Weaken a bad habit by avoiding everything that occasioned it or stimulated it, without concentrating upon it in your zeal to avoid it. Then divert your mind to some good habit and steadily cultivate it until it becomes a dependable part of you.

>We can choose to learn!
>We can choose to grow!
>We can choose to change!

There is a Chinese art named Kaizen. Kaizen is about using the smallest possible step to create the largest possible change. What if instead of exercising for thirty minutes a day you only had to exercise for five? Do you think you'd be more likely to follow an exercise routine that had such a small time investment? What about writing? Would it be easier to start if your goal was only one sentence or a few sentences a day? A sentence a day might seem like a silly goal, but the point is this; it gets your mind flowing. It's the same with exercising five minutes a day. It gets you moving. The magic is to start. Once you're doing something it's easy to build momentum. It always takes more energy to overcome inertia than it does to keep something moving or to speed it up once it's moving.

>So get moving! Start small.
>Just take a step, even if it's a tiny step.

And then take another. Remember, forward motion builds momentum. And momentum creates miracles! One small step you can take is this; ask yourself, "Where do I want to end up?" Or, "What do I want out of life?" You know that what you get out of life depends on what you put into it. You might have the answer to these questions right away. And you might not. That's OK too. If you aren't sure what you want out of life, this process can help. Ask yourself the question again. Only this time tell your mind exactly when you'll be back for the answer— a few hours, the next morning, be specific, then let it pour out in Your Blueprint Journal!

Change so permanent so revenant

"I'm creating something to base my life upon 'Change'

Change so permanent so revenant

Changing goes on and on, in this estrange world
1995 was yet to come, turning nine, I would soon to be
A trip was definite, spending time with distant relative of mine
A celebration in the midst of sorrow, 'A hurricane in range'
A bliss of some sort and pain not to support

Change so permanent so revenant

A soul I didn't want to lose is gone
You were always there to protect me I thought
Now, washed away in distance right next to me
Blind folded was the mirror, how could it see?
One shot of an arrow I thought, I felt before.
Was it you oh hurricane?

CHANGE YOUR BLUEPRINT CHANGE YOUR LIFE

Little Did I Know all would be estrange
Change I did not want to make
Feels as if I am in a lost sea no one to reach no one to see

Change so permanent so revenant

Hopeless would I be, a mother disable, & pregnant on a journey she didn't want to be
A father and his thoughts; where was his mind lost?
Undergoing an enlistment surgery, I thought
Nothing was new or old, all this had once happened
I remember, he said a father now a son
Thoughts are coming in like waves.
The years go by and time disappears, but June was here to stay

Change so permanent so revenant

No one will ever know how I feel.
For I cannot even explain it all.
Nothing remains the same
For now, I am me, myself, and I
What used to be "good days" are now filled with memories.
Tomorrow comes, and then again it goes,
And my ambition to become successful grows and grows.

Around the corner, yet miles away,
The life I want now gets closer each day.
All I've ever wanted was something to live for a change on its way.
I don't want to be this person anymore.

CHANGE YOUR BLUEPRINT THROUGH JOURNALING

Change so permanent so revenant

I've been basing my life upon what others think and create for me
I wish I could go back and redo everything, every time an eye would blink.
I've fought to become who I am and what I want to be.
I have to remind myself that one day I will be free, and be in a new way
Free from the rules I followed as a child,

Change so permanent so revenant

When everything was a game and life was so mild.
Now times have changed and I realize I have to change,
And sometimes it seems like nobody even cares.
It's like no one pays attention to what I feel is best for me,
And what I think about the way some things should be.
I understand now that I'm pretty much on my own,
And I know a lot of what I can do will never be known.

All the time I think about everything I can't say, what I have to keep in,
And by doing this, my thoughts only get more complicated and deepen.
Soon I hope to find out who I am and what I am meant to become.
I want to know where I'm going.

Change so permanent so revenant"

—Minache Eliah-Sawh

CHANGE YOUR BLUEPRINT CHANGE YOUR LIFE

I don't need to be reminded of where I came from. All of us experience change in our lives. Change is the one constant in our lives. There are changes that we look forward to and change that we fear. However, one thing is for sure. Things will not stay the same no matter how much we would like them too. When a life change occurs, we have two choices in how to respond. We can despair that a change has come and assume that things will be worse, or we can look with excitement at the new possibilities that the change is present.

With Divine Love,

CHANGE YOUR BLUEPRINT THROUGH JOURNALING

Date ___/ ___/ _____

Affirmation for today:

This day shall be the best day of my life..

I am Thankful for...

_____
_____
_____

What would make today great?

_____
_____
_____

What is one act of kindness I can do today?

_____

Awesome things that happened today...

_____
_____
_____

What could I have done differently today?

_____
_____

Don't wait until everything is just right. It will never be perfect. There will always be challenges, obstacles and less than perfect conditions. So what! Get started now. With each step you take, you will grow stronger and stronger, more and more skilled, more and more self-confident and more and more successful.

- Mark Victor Hansen

CHANGE YOUR BLUEPRINT, CHANGE YOUR LIFE

Date ___/___/_____

Affirmation for today:

Success is closer than I think.

I am Thankful for...

_____
_____
_____

What would make today great?

_____
_____
_____

What is one act of kindness I can do today?

_____

Awesome things that happened today...

_____
_____
_____

What could I have done differently today?

_____
_____
_____

The greatest mistake you can make in life is to be continually fearing you will make one.

- Elbert Hubbard

CHANGE YOUR BLUEPRINT THROUGH JOURNALING

Date ___/___/_____

Affirmation for today:

I see everything that is happening as designed for my growth and learning.

I am Thankful for...

_____
_____
_____

What would make today great?

_____
_____
_____

What is one act of kindness I can do today?

_____

Awesome things that happened today...

_____
_____
_____

What could I have done differently today?

_____
_____
_____

The eye sees only what the mind is prepared to comprehend.
- Henri Bergson

CHANGE YOUR BLUEPRINT CHANGE YOUR LIFE

Date ___/___/_____

Affirmation for today:

Today I will start with a new determination to Change my Blueprint.

I am Thankful for...

_____
_____
_____

What would make today great?

_____
_____
_____

What is one act of kindness I can do today?

_____

Awesome things that happened today...

_____
_____
_____

What could I have done differently today?

_____
_____
_____

Procrastination is the foundation of all disasters.

- Pandora Poikilos

CHANGE YOUR BLUEPRINT THROUGH JOURNALING

Date ___/___/_____

Affirmation for today:

I allow my life to be huge!

I am Thankful for...

_____
_____
_____

What would make today great?

_____
_____
_____

What is one act of kindness I can do today?

_____

Awesome things that happened today...

_____
_____
_____

What could I have done differently today?

_____
_____
_____

Always Do Your Best: Your best is going to change from moment to moment; it will be different when you are healthy as opposed to sick. Under any circumstance, simply do your best, and you will avoid self-judgment, self-abuse, and regret. - Don Miguel Ruiz

CHANGE YOUR BLUEPRINT CHANGE YOUR LIFE

Date ___/___/_____

Affirmation for today:

I love to focus on the good things in my life and I love that doing this brings me more blessings.

I am Thankful for...

_____
_____
_____

What would make today great?

_____
_____
_____

What is one act of kindness I can do today?

_____

Awesome things that happened today...

_____
_____
_____

What could I have done differently today?

_____
_____
_____

We need to teach the next generation of children from day one that they are responsible for their lives. Mankind's greatest gift, also its greatest curse, is that we have free choice. We can make our choices built from love or from fear. - Elisabeth Kubler-Ross

CHANGE YOUR BLUEPRINT THROUGH JOURNALING

Date ___/___/_____

Affirmation for today:

I learn from all the action I take, which brings me closer to my dreams.

I am Thankful for...

_____
_____
_____

What would make today great?

_____
_____
_____

What is one act of kindness I can do today?

_____

Awesome things that happened today...

_____
_____
_____

What could I have done differently today?

_____
_____
_____

Anyone has a why to live can bear almost any what.
- Friedrich Nietzsche

CHANGE YOUR BLUEPRINT CHANGE YOUR LIFE

Date ___/___/_____

Affirmation for today:

I forgive those who need forgiving for not being what I wanted them to be.

I am Thankful for...

_____
_____
_____

What would make today great?

_____
_____
_____

What is one act of kindness I can do today?

_____

Awesome things that happened today...

_____
_____
_____

What could I have done differently today?

_____
_____
_____

Success is due to our stretching to the challenges of life. Failure comes when we shrink from them.

- John C. Maxwell

CHANGE YOUR BLUEPRINT THROUGH JOURNALING

Date ___/___/_____

Affirmation for today:

I accept that I will fail and see failure as one step closer to success.

I am Thankful for...

_____
_____
_____

What would make today great?

_____
_____
_____

What is one act of kindness I can do today?

_____

Awesome things that happened today...

_____
_____
_____

What could I have done differently today?

_____
_____
_____

Not in his speech, not in his thoughts, I see his greatness, only in his actions, in his life.

- Hermann Hesse

CHANGE YOUR BLUEPRINT CHANGE YOUR LIFE

Date ___/___/_____

Affirmation for today:

I am a co-creator of my life and take responsibility for how I choose to live it!

I am Thankful for...

_____
_____
_____

What would make today great?

_____
_____
_____

What is one act of kindness I can do today?

_____

Awesome things that happened today...

_____
_____
_____

What could I have done differently today?

_____
_____
_____

In every community, there is work to be done. In every nation, there are wounds to heal. In every heart, there is the power to do it.

- Marianne Williamson

CHANGE YOUR BLUEPRINT THROUGH JOURNALING

Date ___/___/_____

Affirmation for today:

I choose to look for the abundance that is already present in my life.

I am Thankful for...

_____
_____
_____

What would make today great?

_____
_____
_____

What is one act of kindness I can do today?

_____

Awesome things that happened today...

_____
_____
_____

What could I have done differently today?

_____
_____
_____

You are so busy being YOU that you have no idea how utterly unprecedented you are.

- John Green

CHANGE YOUR BLUEPRINT CHANGE YOUR LIFE

Date ___/___/_____

Affirmation for today:

I take action in the direction of my desired outcome.

I am Thankful for...

_____
_____
_____

What would make today great?

_____
_____
_____

What is one act of kindness I can do today?

_____

Awesome things that happened today...

_____
_____
_____

What could I have done differently today?

_____
_____
_____

No man is defeated without until he has first been defeated within.

- Eleanor Roosevelt

CHANGE YOUR BLUEPRINT THROUGH JOURNALING

Date ___/___/_____

Affirmation for today:

As I change my thoughts, the world around me changes. The past is over, so it has no power now. The thoughts of this moment create my future.

I am Thankful for...

_____
_____
_____

What would make today great?

_____
_____
_____

What is one act of kindness I can do today?

_____

Awesome things that happened today...

_____
_____
_____

What could I have done differently today?

_____
_____
_____

Even if you be otherwise perfect, you fail without humility.

- The Talmud

CHANGE YOUR BLUEPRINT CHANGE YOUR LIFE

Date ___/___/_____

Affirmation for today:

I am open to even greater things being possible than I can now imagine.

I am Thankful for...

_____
_____
_____

What would make today great?

_____
_____
_____

What is one act of kindness I can do today?

_____

Awesome things that happened today...

_____
_____
_____

What could I have done differently today?

_____
_____
_____

Evaluating the benefits and drawbacks of any relationship is your responsibility. You do not have to passively accept what is brought to you. You can choose.

- Deborah Day

CHANGE YOUR BLUEPRINT THROUGH JOURNALING

Date ___/___/_____

Affirmation for today:

I have the inner strength to handle any situation that I find myself in.

I am Thankful for...

_____
_____
_____

What would make today great?

_____
_____
_____

What is one act of kindness I can do today?

_____

Awesome things that happened today...

_____
_____
_____

What could I have done differently today?

_____
_____
_____

Always do your best. What you plant now, you will harvest later.

- Og Mandino

CHANGE YOUR BLUEPRINT CHANGE YOUR LIFE

Date ___/___/_____

Affirmation for today:

I come from the loving space of my heart, and I know that love opens new possibilities.

I am Thankful for...

_____
_____
_____

What would make today great?

_____
_____
_____

What is one act of kindness I can do today?

_____

Awesome things that happened today...

_____
_____
_____

What could I have done differently today?

_____
_____
_____

Your time is limited, so don't waste it living someone else's life. Don't be trapped by dogma - which is living with the results of other people's thinking. Don't let the noise of others' opinions drown out your own inner voice. And most important, have the courage to follow your heart and intuition. - Steve Jobs

CHANGE YOUR BLUEPRINT THROUGH JOURNALING

Date ___/___/_____

Affirmation for today:

My mind and body are healthy and strong and I nourish them with my spirit, which is infinite.

I am Thankful for...

_____
_____
_____

What would make today great?

_____
_____
_____

What is one act of kindness I can do today?

_____

Awesome things that happened today...

_____
_____
_____

What could I have done differently today?

_____
_____
_____

The truth will set you free, but first it will piss you off.

- Gloria Steinem

CHANGE YOUR BLUEPRINT CHANGE YOUR LIFE

Date ___/___/_____

Affirmation for today:

I let go of what no longer supports me.

I am Thankful for...

_____
_____
_____

What would make today great?

_____
_____
_____

What is one act of kindness I can do today?

_____

Awesome things that happened today...

_____
_____
_____

What could I have done differently today?

_____
_____
_____

I don't believe you have to be better than everybody else. I believe you have to be better than you ever thought you could be.

- Ken Venturi

CHANGE YOUR BLUEPRINT THROUGH JOURNALING

Date ___/___/_____

Affirmation for today:

I accept the past as it is and give up wishing it was better. It was as it was and that is ok with me.

I am Thankful for…

_____
_____
_____

What would make today great?

_____
_____
_____

What is one act of kindness I can do today?

_____

Awesome things that happened today…

_____
_____
_____

What could I have done differently today?

_____
_____
_____

Seeking love keeps you from the awareness that you already have it that you are it.

- Byron Katie

CHANGE YOUR BLUEPRINT CHANGE YOUR LIFE

Date ___/___/_____

Affirmation for today:

The past is over; the future is defined by what I do today.

I am Thankful for...

_____
_____
_____

What would make today great?

_____
_____
_____

What is one act of kindness I can do today?

_____

Awesome things that happened today...

_____
_____
_____

What could I have done differently today?

_____
_____
_____

Love conquers all things; let us surrender to Love.

- Virgil

CHANGE YOUR BLUEPRINT THROUGH JOURNALING

Date ___/___/_____

Affirmation for today:

I am flexible. I welcome changes in my life and adapt with courage and ease.

I am Thankful for...

_____
_____
_____

What would make today great?

_____
_____
_____

What is one act of kindness I can do today?

_____

Awesome things that happened today...

_____
_____
_____

What could I have done differently today?

_____
_____
_____

Lots of people want to ride with you in the limo, but what you want is someone who will take the bus with you when the limo breaks down.

- Oprah Winfrey

CHANGE YOUR BLUEPRINT CHANGE YOUR LIFE

Date ___/ ___/ _____

Affirmation for today:

I practice balance in setting boundaries and helping others. I am here to be of service, to love myself and share that love with others

I am Thankful for...

_____
_____
_____

What would make today great?

_____
_____
_____

What is one act of kindness I can do today?

_____

Awesome things that happened today...

_____
_____
_____

What could I have done differently today?

_____
_____
_____

Creative work is not a selfish act or a bid for attention on the part of the actor. It's a gift to the world and every being in it. Don't cheat us of your contribution. Give us what you've got.

- Steven Pressfield

CHANGE YOUR BLUEPRINT THROUGH JOURNALING

Date ___/ ___/ _____

Affirmation for today:

I allow myself to feel happiness and joy for no reason at all. Simply because I deserve it.

I am Thankful for...

_____
_____
_____

What would make today great?

_____
_____
_____

What is one act of kindness I can do today?

_____

Awesome things that happened today...

_____
_____
_____

What could I have done differently today?

_____
_____
_____

Where you stumble and fall, there you will find gold.

- Joseph Campbell

CHANGE YOUR BLUEPRINT CHANGE YOUR LIFE

Date ___/___/_____

Affirmation for today:

I am worthy of my dreams.

I am Thankful for...

_____
_____
_____

What would make today great?

_____
_____
_____

What is one act of kindness I can do today?

_____

Awesome things that happened today...

_____
_____
_____

What could I have done differently today?

_____
_____
_____

Listen to the mustn'ts, child. Listen to the don'ts. Listen to the shouldn'ts, the impossibles, the won'ts. Listen to the never haves, then listen close to me. Anything can happen, child. Anything can be.

- Shel Silverstein

CHANGE YOUR BLUEPRINT THROUGH JOURNALING

Date ___/ ___/ _____

Affirmation for today:

It's safe for me to be me.

I am Thankful for...

_____
_____
_____

What would make today great?

_____
_____
_____

What is one act of kindness I can do today?

_____

Awesome things that happened today...

_____
_____
_____

What could I have done differently today?

_____
_____
_____

Prosperity is the out-picturing of substance in our affairs. Everything in the Universe is for us. Nothing is against us. Life is ever giving of Itself. We must receive, utilize and extend the gift. Success and prosperity are spiritual attributes belonging to all people, but not necessarily used by all. - Ernest Holmes

CHANGE YOUR BLUEPRINT CHANGE YOUR LIFE

Date ___/___/_____

Affirmation for today:

I am 100% Self-Approved.

I am Thankful for...

_____
_____
_____

What would make today great?

_____
_____
_____

What is one act of kindness I can do today?

_____

Awesome things that happened today...

_____
_____
_____

What could I have done differently today?

_____
_____
_____

Whenever you're in conflict with someone, there is one factor that can make the difference between damaging your relationship and deepening it. That factor is attitude.

- William James

CHANGE YOUR BLUEPRINT THROUGH JOURNALING

Date ___/___/_____

Affirmation for today:

I am the way I see the world.

I am Thankful for...

_____
_____
_____

What would make today great?

_____
_____
_____

What is one act of kindness I can do today?

_____

Awesome things that happened today...

_____
_____
_____

What could I have done differently today?

_____
_____
_____

Do not go where the path may lead, go instead where there is no path and leave a trail.

- Ralph Waldo Emerson

CHANGE YOUR BLUEPRINT CHANGE YOUR LIFE

Date ___/___/_____

Affirmation for today:

I am the one who gets to choose what this means.

I am Thankful for...

_____
_____
_____

What would make today great?

_____
_____
_____

What is one act of kindness I can do today?

_____

Awesome things that happened today...

_____
_____
_____

What could I have done differently today?

_____
_____
_____

We all have within us the ability to move from struggle to grace.

- Arianna Huffington

CHANGE YOUR BLUEPRINT THROUGH JOURNALING

Date ___/___/_____

Affirmation for today:

I take pleasure in my own solitude, because I am comfortable with myself.

I am Thankful for...
_____
_____
_____

What would make today great?
_____
_____
_____

What is one act of kindness I can do today?
_____

Awesome things that happened today...
_____
_____
_____

What could I have done differently today?
_____
_____
_____

Be the one who nurtures and builds. Be the one who has an understanding and a forgiving heart one who looks for the best in people. Leave people better than you found them.

- Marvin J. Ashton

CHANGE YOUR BLUEPRINT CHANGE YOUR LIFE

Date ___/___/_____

Affirmation for today:

I am grateful for this opportunity to learn how to Love even more.

I am Thankful for...

_____
_____
_____

What would make today great?

_____
_____
_____

What is one act of kindness I can do today?

_____

Awesome things that happened today...

_____
_____
_____

What could I have done differently today?

_____
_____
_____

Most of the shadows of this life are caused by standing in one's own sunshine.

- Ralph Waldo Emerson

CHANGE YOUR BLUEPRINT THROUGH JOURNALING

Date ___/___/_____

Affirmation for today:

As I do so, I am supported by The Universe.

I am Thankful for...

_____
_____
_____

What would make today great?

_____
_____
_____

What is one act of kindness I can do today?

_____

Awesome things that happened today...

_____
_____
_____

What could I have done differently today?

_____
_____
_____

When the best leader's work is done the people say: We did it ourselves.

- Lao Tzu

CHANGE YOUR BLUEPRINT CHANGE YOUR LIFE

Date ___/___/_____

Affirmation for today:

I am here to act and learn and get wiser because of it.

I am Thankful for...

_____
_____
_____

What would make today great?

_____
_____
_____

What is one act of kindness I can do today?

_____

Awesome things that happened today...

_____
_____
_____

What could I have done differently today?

_____
_____
_____

Put your heart, mind, and soul into even your smallest acts. This is the secret of success.

- Swami Sivananda

CHANGE YOUR BLUEPRINT THROUGH JOURNALING

Date ___/___/_____

Affirmation for today:

I make a new decision about what's possible in my life.

I am Thankful for...

_____
_____
_____

What would make today great?

_____
_____
_____

What is one act of kindness I can do today?

_____

Awesome things that happened today...

_____
_____
_____

What could I have done differently today?

_____
_____
_____

Courage and willingness to just go for it, trying new things that are scary - it is a really attractive quality.

- Alanis Morissette

CHANGE YOUR BLUEPRINT CHANGE YOUR LIFE

Date ___/___/_____

Affirmation for today:

I embrace my fear of failure.

I am Thankful for...

_____
_____
_____

What would make today great?

_____
_____
_____

What is one act of kindness I can do today?

_____

Awesome things that happened today...

_____
_____
_____

What could I have done differently today?

_____
_____
_____

Yes, I am a dreamer. For a dreamer is one who can find his way by moonlight, and see the dawn before the rest of the world.

- Oscar Wilde

CHANGE YOUR BLUEPRINT THROUGH JOURNALING

Date ___/ ___/ _____

Affirmation for today:

I can feel the love of all those who love me, but are not physically nearby.

I am Thankful for...

_____
_____
_____

What would make today great?

_____
_____
_____

What is one act of kindness I can do today?

_____

Awesome things that happened today...

_____
_____
_____

What could I have done differently today?

_____
_____
_____

Either I will find a way, or I will make one.

- Philip Sidney

CHANGE YOUR BLUEPRINT CHANGE YOUR LIFE

Date ___/___/_____

Affirmation for today:

I am open, free and loving.

I am Thankful for...

_____
_____
_____

What would make today great?

_____
_____
_____

What is one act of kindness I can do today?

_____
_____

Awesome things that happened today...

_____
_____
_____

What could I have done differently today?

_____
_____
_____

Only by its own roots does a tree stand tall and only by its own light does the sun shine brightly and bring life to our world. So it is with you - only when you're trusting, loving and rooted in your true Self will the life that is your highest potential begin to manifest. Only when you are walking on the path of your highest potential will you ever be able to shine brightly and bring light to the darkness in others. —Anon

CHANGE YOUR BLUEPRINT THROUGH JOURNALING

Date ___/___/_____

Affirmation for today:

It's okay for me to ask for help with food.

I am Thankful for...

_____
_____
_____

What would make today great?

_____
_____
_____

What is one act of kindness I can do today?

_____

Awesome things that happened today...

_____
_____
_____

What could I have done differently today?

_____
_____
_____

You will find that it is necessary to let things go; simply for the reason that they are heavy. So let them go, let go of them. I tie no weights to my ankles.

- C. JoyBell

CHANGE YOUR BLUEPRINT CHANGE YOUR LIFE

Date ___/___/_____

Affirmation for today:

I see beyond what is lost to what is being born.

I am Thankful for...

_____
_____
_____

What would make today great?

_____
_____
_____

What is one act of kindness I can do today?

_____

Awesome things that happened today...

_____
_____
_____

What could I have done differently today?

_____
_____
_____

Instead of making up excuses for why something is impossible, it's far better to come up with reasons why it could be possible. One reason why is more powerful than all the reasons why not.

- Jackson Kiddard

CHANGE YOUR BLUEPRINT THROUGH JOURNALING

Date ___/___/_____

Affirmation for today:

I encourage and support others and they do the same for me!

I am Thankful for...

_____
_____
_____

What would make today great?

_____
_____
_____

What is one act of kindness I can do today?

_____

Awesome things that happened today...

_____
_____
_____

What could I have done differently today?

_____
_____
_____

Always do what you are afraid to do.

- Ralph Waldo Emerson

CHANGE YOUR BLUEPRINT CHANGE YOUR LIFE

Date ___/ ___/ _____

Affirmation for today:

I am more than my circumstances.

I am Thankful for...

_____
_____
_____

What would make today great?

_____
_____
_____

What is one act of kindness I can do today?

_____

Awesome things that happened today...

_____
_____
_____

What could I have done differently today?

_____
_____
_____

Life is change. Growth is optional. Choose wisely.

- Anon

CHANGE YOUR BLUEPRINT THROUGH JOURNALING

Date ___/ ___/ _____

Affirmation for today:

My happiness is my responsibility and no one else's.

I am Thankful for...

_____
_____
_____

What would make today great?

_____
_____
_____

What is one act of kindness I can do today?

_____

Awesome things that happened today...

_____
_____
_____

What could I have done differently today?

_____
_____
_____

Life is, at times, tough...And all we need to do is to prove that we are tougher than it...

- Sanhita Baruah

CHANGE YOUR BLUEPRINT CHANGE YOUR LIFE

Date ___/___/_____

Affirmation for today:

Today, I start before I am ready.

I am Thankful for...

_____
_____
_____

What would make today great?

_____
_____
_____

What is one act of kindness I can do today?

_____

Awesome things that happened today...

_____
_____
_____

What could I have done differently today?

_____
_____
_____

Anything that looks like chaos and calamity in your life is just the Universe's way of saying 'Trust me and we'll make a life together that is beyond your wildest dreams.' The key is to trust. There's a bigger vision and purpose inside you that your small brain or Ego can imagine. The Universe has bigger and better plans for you. It's your job to be of service and not get in your own way. You can only receive what you believe. When you trust you open yourself up to greater possibilities outside of your control or imagination. So what's it gunna be? Fear or trust? - Anon

CHANGE YOUR BLUEPRINT THROUGH JOURNALING

Date ___/___/_____

Affirmation for today:

I embrace my inner power and use it in service of Love and light!

I am Thankful for...

_____
_____
_____

What would make today great?

_____
_____
_____

What is one act of kindness I can do today?

_____

Awesome things that happened today...

_____
_____
_____

What could I have done differently today?

_____
_____

Many people think I can't live a normal life because I don't have arms or legs. I could choose to believe that and give up trying. I could stay at home and wait for others to take care of me. Instead, I choose to believe that I can do anything, and I always try to do things my own way. I choose to be happy. I am happy because I am always thankful.

- Nick Vujicic

CHANGE YOUR BLUEPRINT CHANGE YOUR LIFE

Date ___/___/_____

Affirmation for today:

What I offer to the world is as bright as anyone else.

I am Thankful for...

_____
_____
_____

What would make today great?

_____
_____
_____

What is one act of kindness I can do today?

_____

Awesome things that happened today...

_____
_____
_____

What could I have done differently today?

_____
_____
_____

You have to learn the rules of the game. And then you have to play better than anyone else.

- Albert Einstein

CHANGE YOUR BLUEPRINT THROUGH JOURNALING

Date ___/___/_____

Affirmation for today:

I accept all that this present moment contains.

I am Thankful for...

_____
_____
_____

What would make today great?

_____
_____
_____

What is one act of kindness I can do today?

_____

Awesome things that happened today...

_____
_____
_____

What could I have done differently today?

_____
_____
_____

Truth never damages a cause that is just.
- Mahatma Gandhi

CHANGE YOUR BLUEPRINT CHANGE YOUR LIFE

Date ___/___/_____

Affirmation for today:

I celebrate setting healthy boundaries.

I am Thankful for...

_____
_____
_____

What would make today great?

_____
_____
_____

What is one act of kindness I can do today?

_____

Awesome things that happened today...

_____
_____
_____

What could I have done differently today?

_____
_____
_____

If you have time to whine and complain about something then you have the time to do something about it.

- Anthony D'Angelo

CHANGE YOUR BLUEPRINT THROUGH JOURNALING

Date ___/___/_____

Affirmation for today:

I attract relationships and business partnerships that serve my empowerment.

I am Thankful for...

_____
_____
_____

What would make today great?

_____
_____
_____

What is one act of kindness I can do today?

_____

Awesome things that happened today...

_____
_____
_____

What could I have done differently today?

_____
_____
_____

There are more things, Lucilius, that frighten us than injure us, and we suffer more in imagination than in reality.

- Epistulae ad Lucilium

CHANGE YOUR BLUEPRINT CHANGE YOUR LIFE

Date ___/___/_____

Affirmation for today:

I choose to find the empowering meaning in every circumstance.

I am Thankful for...

_____
_____
_____

What would make today great?

_____
_____
_____

What is one act of kindness I can do today?

_____

Awesome things that happened today...

_____
_____
_____

What could I have done differently today?

_____
_____
_____

I'm continually trying to make choices that put me against my own comfort zone. As long as you're uncomfortable, it means you're growing.

- Ashton Kutcher

CHANGE YOUR BLUEPRINT THROUGH JOURNALING

Date ___/___/_____

Affirmation for today:

I trust and act on my intuition in my relationship.

I am Thankful for...

_____
_____
_____

What would make today great?

_____
_____
_____

What is one act of kindness I can do today?

_____

Awesome things that happened today...

_____
_____
_____

What could I have done differently today?

_____
_____
_____

Wisdom comes only when you stop looking for it and start living the life the Creator intended for you.

- Hopi Proverb

CHANGE YOUR BLUEPRINT CHANGE YOUR LIFE

Date ___/___/_____

Affirmation for today:

It's worth losing everything to gain myself.

I am Thankful for...

_____
_____
_____

What would make today great?

_____
_____
_____

What is one act of kindness I can do today?

_____

Awesome things that happened today...

_____
_____
_____

What could I have done differently today?

_____
_____
_____

You must constantly ask yourself these questions: Who am I around? What are they doing to me? What have they got me reading? What have they got me saying? Where do they have me going? What do they have me thinking? And most important, what do they have me becoming? Then ask yourself the big question: Is that okay? Your life does not get better by chance, it gets better by change. - Jim Rohn

CHANGE YOUR BLUEPRINT THROUGH JOURNALING

Date ___/___/_____

Affirmation for today:

Today, I take chances in the direction of my dreams.

I am Thankful for...

_____
_____
_____

What would make today great?

_____
_____
_____

What is one act of kindness I can do today?

_____

Awesome things that happened today...

_____
_____
_____

What could I have done differently today?

_____
_____
_____

Let this truth go as deep in you as possible: that life is already here, arrived. You are standing on the goal. Don't ask about the path.

- Osho

CHANGE YOUR BLUEPRINT CHANGE YOUR LIFE

Date ___/___/_____

Affirmation for today:

I find happiness and fulfillment in myself first!

I am Thankful for...

_____
_____
_____

What would make today great?

_____
_____
_____

What is one act of kindness I can do today?

_____

Awesome things that happened today...

_____
_____
_____

What could I have done differently today?

_____
_____
_____
_____

She took a leap, and built her wings on the way down.

- Anon

CHANGE YOUR BLUEPRINT THROUGH JOURNALING

Date ___/ ___/ _____

Affirmation for today:

I may not understand what's good about this situation, but there is good here.

I am Thankful for...

_____
_____
_____

What would make today great?

_____
_____
_____

What is one act of kindness I can do today?

_____

Awesome things that happened today...

_____
_____
_____

What could I have done differently today?

_____
_____
_____

The greatest of human emotions is love. The most valuable of human gifts is the ability to learn. Therefore, learn to love.

- UJ Ramdas

CHANGE YOUR BLUEPRINT CHANGE YOUR LIFE

Date ___/___/_____

Affirmation for today:

I am here to add value to the world, not to get approval from the world.

I am Thankful for...

_____
_____
_____

What would make today great?

_____
_____
_____

What is one act of kindness I can do today?

_____

Awesome things that happened today...

_____
_____
_____

What could I have done differently today?

_____
_____
_____

Once you choose hope, anything's possible.

- Christopher Reeve

CHANGE YOUR BLUEPRINT THROUGH JOURNALING

Date ___/___/_____

Affirmation for today:

There is no lack. When others succeed it takes nothing from me.

I am Thankful for...

_____
_____
_____

What would make today great?

_____
_____
_____

What is one act of kindness I can do today?

_____

Awesome things that happened today...

_____
_____
_____

What could I have done differently today?

_____
_____
_____

Positive anything is better than negative nothing.

- Elbert Hubbard

CHANGE YOUR BLUEPRINT CHANGE YOUR LIFE

Date ___/___/_____

Affirmation for today:

My body is beautiful, and I love and nurture it.

I am Thankful for...
_____
_____
_____

What would make today great?
_____
_____
_____

What is one act of kindness I can do today?
_____

Awesome things that happened today...
_____
_____
_____

What could I have done differently today?
_____
_____
_____

Every addiction arises from an unconscious refusal to face and move through your own pain. Every addiction starts with pain and ends with pain. Whatever the substance you are addicted to - alcohol, food, legal or illegal drugs, or a person - you are using something or somebody to cover up your pain. - Eckhart Tolle

CHANGE YOUR BLUEPRINT THROUGH JOURNALING

Date ___/___/_____

Affirmation for today:

I have the courage to take this head on.

I am Thankful for...

_____
_____
_____

What would make today great?

_____
_____
_____

What is one act of kindness I can do today?

_____

Awesome things that happened today...

_____
_____
_____

What could I have done differently today?

_____
_____
_____

There are only two lasting bequests we can hope to give our children. One of these is roots, the other, wings.

- Johann Wolfgang von Goethe

CHANGE YOUR BLUEPRINT CHANGE YOUR LIFE

Date ___/___/_____

Affirmation for today:

I give up the right to criticize myself.

I am Thankful for...

_____
_____
_____

What would make today great?

_____
_____
_____

What is one act of kindness I can do today?

_____

Awesome things that happened today...

_____
_____
_____

What could I have done differently today?

_____
_____
_____

Do not attempt to do a thing unless you are sure of yourself, but do not relinquish it simply because someone else is not sure of you.

- Stewart E. White

CHANGE YOUR BLUEPRINT THROUGH JOURNALING

Date ___/ ___/ _____

Affirmation for today:

I move through forgiveness to love.

I am Thankful for...

_____
_____
_____

What would make today great?

_____
_____
_____

What is one act of kindness I can do today?

_____

Awesome things that happened today...

_____
_____
_____

What could I have done differently today?

_____
_____
_____

Believe that life is worth living and your belief will help create the fact.
- William James

CHANGE YOUR BLUEPRINT CHANGE YOUR LIFE

Date ___/___/_____

Affirmation for today:

I love who I am.

I am Thankful for...

_____
_____
_____

What would make today great?

_____
_____
_____

What is one act of kindness I can do today?

_____

Awesome things that happened today...

_____
_____
_____

What could I have done differently today?

_____
_____
_____

I've come to believe that all my past failure and frustration were actually laying the foundation for the understandings that have created the new level of living I now enjoy.

- Tony Robbins

CHANGE YOUR BLUEPRINT THROUGH JOURNALING

Date ___/___/_____

Affirmation for today:

I have personal magnetism.

I am Thankful for...

_____
_____
_____

What would make today great?

_____
_____

What is one act of kindness I can do today?

_____

Awesome things that happened today...

_____
_____
_____

What could I have done differently today?

_____
_____
_____

There is overwhelming evidence that the higher the level of self-esteem, the more likely one will treat others with respect, kindness, and generosity. People who do not experience self-love have little or no capacity to love others.

- Nathaniel Branden

CHANGE YOUR BLUEPRINT CHANGE YOUR LIFE

Date ___/___/_____

Affirmation for today:

I keep my word about my dream schedule.

I am Thankful for...

_____
_____
_____

What would make today great?

_____
_____
_____

What is one act of kindness I can do today?

_____

Awesome things that happened today...

_____
_____
_____

What could I have done differently today?

_____
_____
_____

You're lucky enough to be different, never change.

- Taylor Swift

CHANGE YOUR BLUEPRINT THROUGH JOURNALING

Date ___/___/_____

Affirmation for today:

I live and let live, trusting that The Divine has everyone's best interests in mind, including my own.

I am Thankful for...
_____
_____
_____

What would make today great?
_____
_____
_____

What is one act of kindness I can do today?
_____

Awesome things that happened today...
_____
_____
_____

What could I have done differently today?
_____
_____
_____

Man is a genius when he is dreaming.

— Akira Kurosawa

CHANGE YOUR BLUEPRINT CHANGE YOUR LIFE

Date ___/___/_____

Affirmation for today:

I apply myself fully today.

I am Thankful for...

_____
_____
_____

What would make today great?

_____
_____
_____

What is one act of kindness I can do today?

_____

Awesome things that happened today...

_____
_____
_____

What could I have done differently today?

_____
_____
_____

In the mist of difficulty lies Opportunity.

- Oprah Winfrey

CHANGE YOUR BLUEPRINT THROUGH JOURNALING

Date ___/___/_____

Affirmation for today:

I approve of myself and feel great.

I am Thankful for...

_____
_____
_____

What would make today great?

_____
_____
_____

What is one act of kindness I can do today?

_____

Awesome things that happened today...

_____
_____
_____

What could I have done differently today?

_____
_____
_____

The only answer we have in our life is our attitude and that makes all the difference.

- Mimi Ikonn

CHANGE YOUR BLUEPRINT CHANGE YOUR LIFE

Date ___/___/_____

Affirmation for today:

I celebrate the journey, not the outcome.

I am Thankful for...

_____
_____
_____

What would make today great?

_____
_____
_____

What is one act of kindness I can do today?

_____

Awesome things that happened today...

_____
_____
_____

What could I have done differently today?

_____
_____
_____

Whoever envies another confesses his superiority.

- Samuel Johnson

CHANGE YOUR BLUEPRINT THROUGH JOURNALING

Date ___/___/_____

Affirmation for today:

I celebrate taking steps towards my empowerment and let go of what no longer fits.

I am Thankful for...
_____
_____
_____

What would make today great?
_____
_____
_____

What is one act of kindness I can do today?
_____

Awesome things that happened today...
_____
_____
_____

What could I have done differently today?
_____
_____
_____

The vision must be followed by the venture. It is not enough to stare up the steps - we must step up the stairs.

- Vance Havner

CHANGE YOUR BLUEPRINT CHANGE YOUR LIFE

Date ___/___/_____

Affirmation for today:

I welcome Love with open arms.

I am Thankful for...

_____
_____
_____

What would make today great?

_____
_____
_____

What is one act of kindness I can do today?

_____

Awesome things that happened today...

_____
_____
_____

What could I have done differently today?

_____
_____
_____

No matter what you're going through, there's a light at the end of the tunnel and it may seem hard to get to it but you can do it and just keep working towards it and you'll find the positive side of things.

- Demi Lovato

CHANGE YOUR BLUEPRINT THROUGH JOURNALING

Date ___/___/_____

Affirmation for today:

I remember that I am whole.

I am Thankful for...

_____
_____
_____

What would make today great?

_____
_____
_____

What is one act of kindness I can do today?

_____

Awesome things that happened today...

_____
_____
_____

What could I have done differently today?

_____
_____
_____

Don't Make Assumptions: Find the courage to ask questions and to express what you really want. Communicate with others as clearly as you can to avoid misunderstandings, sadness, and drama. With just this one agreement, you can completely transform your life.

- Don Miguel Ruiz

CHANGE YOUR BLUEPRINT CHANGE YOUR LIFE

Date ___/___/_____

Affirmation for today:

I am a gift, to my family, my friends and my community and I take actions to improve all of them.

I am Thankful for...

_____
_____
_____

What would make today great?

_____
_____
_____

What is one act of kindness I can do today?

_____

Awesome things that happened today...

_____
_____
_____

What could I have done differently today?

_____
_____
_____

Success is often achieved by those who don't know that failure is inevitable.

- Coco Chanel

CHANGE YOUR BLUEPRINT THROUGH JOURNALING

Date ___/___/_____

Affirmation for today:

I am happy with myself, and my circumstances.

I am Thankful for...

_____
_____
_____

What would make today great?

_____
_____
_____

What is one act of kindness I can do today?

_____

Awesome things that happened today...

_____
_____
_____

What could I have done differently today?

_____
_____
_____

Ignorance is bliss... 'til you get screwed!

- UJ Ramdas

CHANGE YOUR BLUEPRINT CHANGE YOUR LIFE

Date ___/___/_____

Affirmation for today:

It is now safe for me to release all past traumas and move into love.

I am Thankful for...

_____
_____
_____

What would make today great?

_____
_____
_____

What is one act of kindness I can do today?

_____

Awesome things that happened today...

_____
_____
_____

What could I have done differently today?

_____
_____
_____

You cannot hate, argue, reason, fight, complain or yell at a dark room enough to illuminate it - only by shining a Light is darkness overcome. Be that Light.

- Anon

CHANGE YOUR BLUEPRINT THROUGH JOURNALING

Date ___/___/_____

Affirmation for today:

My charming personality draws others to me.

I am Thankful for...

_____
_____
_____

What would make today great?

_____
_____
_____

What is one act of kindness I can do today?

_____

Awesome things that happened today...

_____
_____
_____

What could I have done differently today?

_____
_____
_____

What anyone else has or does not have has nothing to do with you. The only thing that affects your experience is the way you utilize the Non-Physical Energy with your thought. Your abundance or lack of it in your experience has nothing to do with what anybody else is doing or having. It has only to do with your perspective.

It has only to do with your offering of thought. If you want your fortunes to shift, you have to begin telling a different story. - Esther Abraham-Hicks

CHANGE YOUR BLUEPRINT CHANGE YOUR LIFE

Date ___/___/_____

Affirmation for today:

I am blessed with many talents.

I am Thankful for...

_____
_____
_____

What would make today great?

_____
_____
_____

What is one act of kindness I can do today?

_____

Awesome things that happened today...

_____
_____
_____

What could I have done differently today?

_____
_____
_____

Communication is the single most important part of creating a healthy relationship. A relationship without communication is like a beautiful flower without water and sunlight, it will quickly wither and die. I don't care if you think what you have to say is hurtful or you are afraid of expressing yourself, speak your Truth. Be kind, but speak up and be honest. It's easy to communicate when it's good news and happy times, but it takes a truly authentic and courageous person to communicate openly and honestly when darkness falls on a relationship. - Jackson Kiddard

CHANGE YOUR BLUEPRINT THROUGH JOURNALING

Date ___/___/_____

Affirmation for today:

I love and appreciate the members of my family.

I am Thankful for...

_____
_____
_____

What would make today great?

_____
_____
_____

What is one act of kindness I can do today?

_____

Awesome things that happened today...

_____
_____
_____

What could I have done differently today?

_____
_____
_____

You can't forgive without loving. And I don't mean sentimentality. I don't mean mush. I mean having enough courage to stand up and say, 'I forgive. I'm finished with it."

- Maya Angelou

CHANGE YOUR BLUEPRINT CHANGE YOUR LIFE

Date ___/ ___/ _____

Affirmation for today:

I celebrate becoming even more of myself today as I let go of what was and step into who I am now.

I am Thankful for...

_____
_____
_____

What would make today great?

_____
_____
_____

What is one act of kindness I can do today?

_____

Awesome things that happened today...

_____
_____
_____

What could I have done differently today?

_____
_____
_____

Always desire to learn something useful.

- Sophocles

CHANGE YOUR BLUEPRINT THROUGH JOURNALING

Date ___/___/_____

Affirmation for today:

I trust my desires and I choose to be aligned with them.

I am Thankful for...

_____
_____
_____

What would make today great?

_____
_____
_____

What is one act of kindness I can do today?

_____

Awesome things that happened today...

_____
_____
_____

What could I have done differently today?

_____
_____
_____

There's nothing more daring than showing up, putting ourselves out there and letting ourselves be seen.

- Sophocles

CHANGE YOUR BLUEPRINT CHANGE YOUR LIFE

Date ___/___/_____

Affirmation for today:

I take Life one step at a time.

I am Thankful for...

_____
_____
_____

What would make today great?

_____
_____
_____

What is one act of kindness I can do today?

_____

Awesome things that happened today...

_____
_____
_____

What could I have done differently today?

_____
_____
_____

Any fact facing us is not as important as our attitude toward it, for that determines our success or failure.

- Norman Vincent Peale

CHANGE YOUR BLUEPRINT THROUGH JOURNALING

Date ___/___/_____

Affirmation for today:

I am unique, special and today I choose to believe in myself.

I am Thankful for...

_____
_____
_____

What would make today great?

_____
_____
_____

What is one act of kindness I can do today?

_____

Awesome things that happened today...

_____
_____
_____

What could I have done differently today?

_____
_____
_____

Patience child, patience. Remember, life is a journey. If you got everything you wanted all at once there'd be no point to living. Enjoy the ride, and in the end you'll see these 'setbacks' as giant leaps forward, only you couldn't see the bigger picture in the moment. Remain calm, all is within reach; all you have to do is show up every day, stay true to your path and you will surely find the treasure you seek. - Jackson Kiddard

CHANGE YOUR BLUEPRINT CHANGE YOUR LIFE

Date ___/___/_____

Affirmation for today:

I get to decide what things mean in my life.

I am Thankful for...

_____
_____
_____

What would make today great?

_____
_____
_____

What is one act of kindness I can do today?

_____

Awesome things that happened today...

_____
_____
_____

What could I have done differently today?

_____
_____
_____

In any situation, the best thing you can do is the right thing; the next best thing you can do is the wrong thing; the worst thing you can do is nothing.

- Theodore Roosevelt

CHANGE YOUR BLUEPRINT THROUGH JOURNALING

Date ___/___/_____

Affirmation for today:

I let go of anything or anyone who prevents me from shining.

I am Thankful for...

_____
_____
_____

What would make today great?

_____
_____
_____

What is one act of kindness I can do today?

_____

Awesome things that happened today...

_____
_____
_____

What could I have done differently today?

_____
_____
_____

Do not wait to strike till the iron is hot; but make it hot by striking.

  - William B. Sprague

CHANGE YOUR BLUEPRINT CHANGE YOUR LIFE

Date ___/___/_____

Affirmation for today:

I am the architect of my life; I build its foundation and choose its contents.

I am Thankful for...

_____
_____
_____

What would make today great?

_____
_____
_____

What is one act of kindness I can do today?

_____

Awesome things that happened today...

_____
_____
_____

What could I have done differently today?

_____
_____
_____

Journal writing is a voyage to the interior.
- Christina Baldwin

CHANGE YOUR BLUEPRINT THROUGH JOURNALING

Date ___/___/_____

Affirmation for today:

Today, I am brimming with energy and overflowing with joy.

I am Thankful for...
_____
_____
_____

What would make today great?
_____
_____
_____

What is one act of kindness I can do today?
_____

Awesome things that happened today...
_____
_____
_____

What could I have done differently today?
_____
_____
_____

You are now at a crossroads. This is your opportunity to make the most important decision you will ever make. Forget your past. Who are you now? Who have you decided you really are now? Don't think about who you have been. Who are you now? Who have you decided to become? Make this decision consciously. Make it carefully. Make it powerfully.

- Tony Robbins

CHANGE YOUR BLUEPRINT CHANGE YOUR LIFE

Date ___/___/_____

Affirmation for today:

Today I will refuse to jump into the middle of others' affairs, issues, and relationships. I will trust others to work out their own problems, including the ideas and feelings they want to communicate to each other.

I am Thankful for...

_____
_____
_____

What would make today great?

_____
_____
_____

What is one act of kindness I can do today?

_____

Awesome things that happened today...

_____
_____
_____

What could I have done differently today?

_____
_____
_____

Yesterday is not ours to recover, but tomorrow is ours to win or lose.

- Lyndon B. Johnson

CHANGE YOUR BLUEPRINT THROUGH JOURNALING

Date ___/___/_____

Affirmation for today:

I am open to love again.

I am Thankful for...

_____
_____
_____

What would make today great?

_____
_____
_____

What is one act of kindness I can do today?

_____

Awesome things that happened today...

_____
_____
_____

What could I have done differently today?

_____
_____
_____

Exploring the unknown requires tolerating uncertainty.
- William Congreve

CHANGE YOUR BLUEPRINT CHANGE YOUR LIFE

Date ___/___/_____

Affirmation for today:

I am superior to negative thoughts and low actions.

I am Thankful for...

_____
_____
_____

What would make today great?

_____
_____
_____

What is one act of kindness I can do today?

_____

Awesome things that happened today...

_____
_____
_____

What could I have done differently today?

_____
_____
_____

Efficiency is doing things right; effectiveness is doing the right things.

- Tim Ferriss

CHANGE YOUR BLUEPRINT THROUGH JOURNALING

Date ___/___/_____

Affirmation for today:

I am worthy of happiness. I choose what makes me happy today.

I am Thankful for...

_____
_____
_____

What would make today great?

_____
_____
_____

What is one act of kindness I can do today?

_____

Awesome things that happened today...

_____
_____
_____

What could I have done differently today?

_____
_____
_____

The hardships that I encountered in the past will help me succeed in the future.

- Philip Emeagwali

CHANGE YOUR BLUEPRINT CHANGE YOUR LIFE

Date ___/___/_____

Affirmation for today:

I have been given endless talents which I begin to utilize today.

I am Thankful for...

_____
_____
_____

What would make today great?

_____
_____
_____

What is one act of kindness I can do today?

_____

Awesome things that happened today...

_____
_____
_____

What could I have done differently today?

_____
_____
_____

Not only do self-love and love of others go hand in hand but ultimately they are indistinguishable.

- M. Scott Peck

CHANGE YOUR BLUEPRINT THROUGH JOURNALING

Date ___/ ___/ _____

Affirmation for today:

I am now ready to accept a happy, fulfilling relationship.

I am Thankful for...

_____
_____
_____

What would make today great?

_____
_____
_____

What is one act of kindness I can do today?

_____

Awesome things that happened today...

_____
_____
_____

What could I have done differently today?

_____
_____
_____

Only by its own roots does a tree stand tall and only by its own light does the sun shine brightly and bring life to our world. So it is with you - only when you're trusting, loving and rooted in your true Self will the life that is your highest potential begin to manifest. Only when you are walking on the path of your highest potential will you ever be able to shine brightly and bring light to the darkness in others. - Anon

CHANGE YOUR BLUEPRINT CHANGE YOUR LIFE

Date ___/___/_____

Affirmation for today:

I forgive those who have harmed me in my past and peacefully detach from them.

I am Thankful for...
_____
_____
_____

What would make today great?
_____
_____
_____

What is one act of kindness I can do today?
_____

Awesome things that happened today...
_____
_____
_____

What could I have done differently today?
_____
_____
_____

The last, if not the greatest, of the human freedoms: to choose their own attitude in any given circumstance.

- Bruno Bettelheim

CHANGE YOUR BLUEPRINT THROUGH JOURNALING

Date ___/___/_____

Affirmation for today:

I trust the voice of the Divine within me.

I am Thankful for...

_____
_____
_____

What would make today great?

_____
_____
_____

What is one act of kindness I can do today?

_____

Awesome things that happened today...

_____
_____
_____

What could I have done differently today?

_____
_____
_____

All of the Great Teachers throughout the history of our species have merely taught one thing, over and over, in whatever language, at whatever time. All have said, simply: Give up weak attractors for strong attractors.

- David Hawkins

CHANGE YOUR BLUEPRINT CHANGE YOUR LIFE

Date ___/___/_____

Affirmation for today:

A river of compassion washes away my anger and replaces it with love.

I am Thankful for...

_____
_____
_____

What would make today great?

_____
_____
_____

What is one act of kindness I can do today?

_____

Awesome things that happened today...

_____
_____
_____

What could I have done differently today?

_____
_____
_____

We choose what attitudes we have right now. And it's a continuing choice.
- John C. Maxwell

CHANGE YOUR BLUEPRINT THROUGH JOURNALING

Date ___/___/_____

Affirmation for today:

I choose to compare myself to all that I can become, and my own light in the world.

I am Thankful for...

_____
_____
_____

What would make today great?

_____
_____
_____

What is one act of kindness I can do today?

_____

Awesome things that happened today...

_____
_____
_____

What could I have done differently today?

_____
_____
_____

The weak can never forgive. Forgiveness is the attribute of the strong.
- Mahatma Gandhi

CHANGE YOUR BLUEPRINT CHANGE YOUR LIFE

Date ___/___/_____

Affirmation for today:

I am guided in my every step by Spirit who leads me towards what I must know and do.

I am Thankful for...

_____
_____
_____

What would make today great?

_____
_____
_____

What is one act of kindness I can do today?

_____

Awesome things that happened today...

_____
_____
_____

What could I have done differently today?

_____
_____
_____

When you choose Love your options narrow because you have chosen to walk a narrower path of trusting your intuition and feelings over the five senses. You cannot seek for Love, since you can only have what already are. And if you have Love this means you must give it away with no expectation of return. Any expectation of return is not love, but the fear of not having love creeping back in. - Jackson Kiddard

CHANGE YOUR BLUEPRINT THROUGH JOURNALING

Date ___/___/_____

Affirmation for today:

I am worthy and deserving of care and attention.

I am Thankful for...

_____
_____
_____

What would make today great?

_____
_____
_____

What is one act of kindness I can do today?

_____

Awesome things that happened today...

_____
_____
_____

What could I have done differently today?

_____
_____
_____

They will always tell you that you can't do what you want to do, but you can do what you want to do. You just have to believe in yourself. The system is to bring you down, but you can rise up.

- ? Bob Marley

CHANGE YOUR BLUEPRINT CHANGE YOUR LIFE

Date ___/___/_____

Affirmation for today:

I possess the qualities needed to be extremely successful.

I am Thankful for...

_____
_____
_____

What would make today great?

_____
_____
_____

What is one act of kindness I can do today?

_____

Awesome things that happened today...

_____
_____
_____

What could I have done differently today?

_____
_____
_____

In the process of letting go you will lose many things from the past, but you will find yourself.

- Deepak Chopra

CHANGE YOUR BLUEPRINT THROUGH JOURNALING

Date ____/____/_____

Affirmation for today:

I am so grateful to have loving, supportive family and friends.

I am Thankful for...

_____
_____
_____

What would make today great?

_____
_____
_____

What is one act of kindness I can do today?

_____

Awesome things that happened today...

_____
_____
_____

What could I have done differently today?

_____
_____
_____

Forgiveness is the fragrance that the violet sheds on the heel that has crushed it.
- Mark Twain

CHANGE YOUR BLUEPRINT CHANGE YOUR LIFE

Date ___/___/_____

Affirmation for today:

Creative energy surges through me and leads me to new and brilliant ideas.

I am Thankful for...

_____
_____
_____

What would make today great?

_____
_____
_____

What is one act of kindness I can do today?

_____

Awesome things that happened today...

_____
_____
_____

What could I have done differently today?

_____
_____
_____

A goal is not always meant to be reached, it often serves simply as something to aim at.

- Bruce Lee

CHANGE YOUR BLUEPRINT THROUGH JOURNALING

Date ___/___/_____

Affirmation for today:

The more love I use and give, the more I have to give, the supply is endless.

I am Thankful for...

_____
_____
_____

What would make today great?

_____
_____
_____

What is one act of kindness I can do today?

_____

Awesome things that happened today...

_____
_____
_____

What could I have done differently today?

_____
_____
_____

Daring to set boundaries is about having the courage to love ourselves, even when we risk disappointing others.

- Brene Brown

CHANGE YOUR BLUEPRINT CHANGE YOUR LIFE

Date ___/ ___/ _____

Affirmation for today:

I surrender my life to my Heart.

I am Thankful for...

_____
_____
_____

What would make today great?

_____
_____
_____

What is one act of kindness I can do today?

_____

Awesome things that happened today...

_____
_____
_____

What could I have done differently today?

_____
_____
_____

Obstacles don't have to stop you. If you run into a wall, don't turn around and give up. Figure out how to climb it, go through it, or work around it.

- Michael Jordan

CHANGE YOUR BLUEPRINT THROUGH JOURNALING

Date ___/___/_____

Affirmation for today:

Happiness is a choice. I base my happiness on my own accomplishments and the blessings I've been given.

I am Thankful for...

_____
_____
_____

What would make today great?

_____
_____
_____

What is one act of kindness I can do today?

_____

Awesome things that happened today...

_____
_____
_____

What could I have done differently today?

_____
_____
_____

The simple intention to surrender control is all you need to experience miracles.

- Gabrielle Bernstein

CHANGE YOUR BLUEPRINT CHANGE YOUR LIFE

Date ___/___/_____

Affirmation for today:

I have no right to compare myself to anyone else, they have their own path.

I am Thankful for...

_____
_____
_____

What would make today great?

_____
_____
_____

What is one act of kindness I can do today?

_____

Awesome things that happened today...

_____
_____
_____

What could I have done differently today?

_____
_____
_____

You can only be jealous of someone who has something you think you ought to have yourself.

- Margaret Atwood

CHANGE YOUR BLUEPRINT THROUGH JOURNALING

Date ___/___/_____

Affirmation for today:

My ability to conquer my challenges is limitless; my potential to succeed is infinite.

I am Thankful for...

_____
_____
_____

What would make today great?

_____
_____
_____

What is one act of kindness I can do today?

_____

Awesome things that happened today...

_____
_____
_____

What could I have done differently today?

_____
_____
_____

Being deeply loved by someone gives you strength, while loving someone deeply gives you courage.

- Lao Tzu

CHANGE YOUR BLUEPRINT CHANGE YOUR LIFE

Date ___/___/_____

Affirmation for today:

I choose to find the lesson in my pain.

I am Thankful for...

_____
_____
_____

What would make today great?

_____
_____
_____

What is one act of kindness I can do today?

_____

Awesome things that happened today...

_____
_____
_____

What could I have done differently today?

_____
_____
_____

For my part, I travel not to go anywhere, but to go. I travel for travel's sake. The great affair is to move.

- Robert Louis Stevenson

CHANGE YOUR BLUEPRINT THROUGH JOURNALING

Date ___/___/_____

Affirmation for today:

I focus on what I can control and give it an empowering meaning.

I am Thankful for...

_____
_____
_____

What would make today great?

_____
_____
_____

What is one act of kindness I can do today?

_____

Awesome things that happened today...

_____
_____
_____

What could I have done differently today?

_____
_____
_____

A ship in harbor is safe, but that is not what ships are built for.
- John A. Shedd

CHANGE YOUR BLUEPRINT CHANGE YOUR LIFE

Date ___/___/_____

Affirmation for today:

I deserve to be employed and paid well for my time, efforts, and ideas. Each day, I am closer to finding the perfect job for me.

I am Thankful for...

_____
_____
_____

What would make today great?

_____
_____
_____

What is one act of kindness I can do today?

_____

Awesome things that happened today...

_____
_____
_____

What could I have done differently today?

_____
_____
_____

Lying is done with words and also with silence.

- Adrienne Rich

CHANGE YOUR BLUEPRINT THROUGH JOURNALING

Date ___/___/_____

Affirmation for today:

The use of love makes me feel good; it is an expression of my inner joy.

I am Thankful for...

_____
_____
_____

What would make today great?

_____
_____
_____

What is one act of kindness I can do today?

_____

Awesome things that happened today...

_____
_____
_____

What could I have done differently today?

_____
_____
_____

Getting ahead in a difficult profession requires avid faith in yourself. That is why some people with mediocre talent, but with great inner drive, go much further than people with vastly superior talent.

- Sophia Loren

CHANGE YOUR BLUEPRINT CHANGE YOUR LIFE

Date ___/___/_____

Affirmation for today:

I can make the right decisions, because I draw from my inner strength.

I am Thankful for...
_____
_____
_____

What would make today great?
_____
_____
_____

What is one act of kindness I can do today?
_____

Awesome things that happened today...
_____
_____
_____

What could I have done differently today?
_____
_____
_____

What lies behind us and what lies ahead of us are tiny matters compared to what lies within us.

- Ralph Waldo Emerson

CHANGE YOUR BLUEPRINT THROUGH JOURNALING

Date ___/___/_____

Affirmation for today:

I am courageous and I stand up for myself.

I am Thankful for...

_____
_____
_____

What would make today great?

_____
_____
_____

What is one act of kindness I can do today?

_____

Awesome things that happened today...

_____
_____
_____

What could I have done differently today?

_____
_____
_____

Most of the important things in the world have been accomplished by people who have kept on trying when there seemed to be no hope at all.

- Dale Carnegie

CHANGE YOUR BLUEPRINT CHANGE YOUR LIFE

Date ___/___/____

Affirmation for today:

The more I love myself, the more I love people.

I am Thankful for...

_____
_____
_____

What would make today great?

_____
_____
_____

What is one act of kindness I can do today?

_____

Awesome things that happened today...

_____
_____
_____

What could I have done differently today?

_____
_____
_____

Have patience. All things are difficult before they become easy.

- Saadi

CHANGE YOUR BLUEPRINT THROUGH JOURNALING

Date ___/___/_____

Affirmation for today:

All is happening in perfect time.

I am Thankful for...
_____
_____
_____

What would make today great?
_____
_____
_____

What is one act of kindness I can do today?
_____

Awesome things that happened today...
_____
_____
_____

What could I have done differently today?
_____
_____
_____

Even a happy life cannot be without a measure of darkness, and the word happy would lose its meaning if it were not balanced by sadness. It is far better take things as they come along with patience and equanimity.

- Carl Jung

CHANGE YOUR BLUEPRINT CHANGE YOUR LIFE

Date ___/___/_____

Affirmation for today:

I choose my response to my circumstances.

I am Thankful for...

_____
_____
_____

What would make today great?

_____
_____
_____

What is one act of kindness I can do today?

_____

Awesome things that happened today...

_____
_____
_____

What could I have done differently today?

_____
_____
_____

If you don't like how things are, change it. You are not a tree.

- Jim Rohn

CHANGE YOUR BLUEPRINT THROUGH JOURNALING

Date ___/___/_____

Affirmation for today:

My thoughts are filled with positivity and my life is plentiful with prosperity.

I am Thankful for...

_____
_____
_____

What would make today great?

_____
_____
_____

What is one act of kindness I can do today?

_____

Awesome things that happened today...

_____
_____
_____

What could I have done differently today?

_____
_____
_____

Take up one idea. Make that one idea your life – think of it, dream of it, live on idea. Let the brain, muscles, nerves, every part of your body be full of that idea, and just leave every other idea alone. This is the way to success. - Swami Vivekananda

CHANGE YOUR BLUEPRINT CHANGE YOUR LIFE

Date ___/___/_____

Affirmation for today:

I choose to begin again each and every day.

I am Thankful for...

_____
_____
_____

What would make today great?

_____
_____
_____

What is one act of kindness I can do today?

_____

Awesome things that happened today...

_____
_____
_____

What could I have done differently today?

_____
_____
_____

Anything is possible as long as you have the passion.

- Guy Forget

CHANGE YOUR BLUEPRINT THROUGH JOURNALING

Date ___/___/____

Affirmation for today:

I'm safe to make new moves and learn as I go.

I am Thankful for...

_____
_____
_____

What would make today great?

_____
_____
_____

What is one act of kindness I can do today?

_____

Awesome things that happened today...

_____
_____
_____

What could I have done differently today?

_____
_____
_____

When we are no longer able to change a situation, we are challenged to change ourselves.

- Viktor E. Frankl

CHANGE YOUR BLUEPRINT CHANGE YOUR LIFE

Date ___/___/_____

Affirmation for today:

The squeeze is good for me.

I am Thankful for...

_____
_____
_____

What would make today great?

_____
_____
_____

What is one act of kindness I can do today?

_____

Awesome things that happened today...

_____
_____
_____

What could I have done differently today?

_____
_____
_____

We cultivate love when we allow our most vulnerable and powerful selves to be deeply seen and known, and when we honor the spiritual connection that grows from that offering with trust, respect, kindness and affection.

- Brene Brown

CHANGE YOUR BLUEPRINT THROUGH JOURNALING

Date ___/___/_____

Affirmation for today:

I choose to ask for help.

I am Thankful for...

_____
_____
_____

What would make today great?

_____
_____
_____

What is one act of kindness I can do today?

_____

Awesome things that happened today...

_____
_____
_____

What could I have done differently today?

_____
_____
_____

To see things in the seed, that is genius.

- Lao Tzu

CHANGE YOUR BLUEPRINT CHANGE YOUR LIFE

Date ___/___/_____

Affirmation for today:

I trust that as I follow my bliss, I will be supported.

I am Thankful for...

_____
_____
_____

What would make today great?

_____
_____
_____

What is one act of kindness I can do today?

_____

Awesome things that happened today...

_____
_____
_____

What could I have done differently today?

_____
_____
_____

Stillness is the key to success.

- Gabrielle Bernstein

CHANGE YOUR BLUEPRINT THROUGH JOURNALING

Date ___/___/_____

Affirmation for today:

Today, I abandon my old habits and take up new, more positive ones.

I am Thankful for...
_____
_____
_____

What would make today great?
_____
_____
_____

What is one act of kindness I can do today?
_____

Awesome things that happened today...
_____
_____
_____

What could I have done differently today?
_____
_____
_____

Trust yourself, then you will know how to live.

- Johann Wolfgang von Goethe

CHANGE YOUR BLUEPRINT CHANGE YOUR LIFE

Date ___/___/_____

Affirmation for today:

Many people look up to me and recognize my worth; I am admired.

I am Thankful for...

_____
_____
_____

What would make today great?

_____
_____
_____

What is one act of kindness I can do today?

_____

Awesome things that happened today...

_____
_____
_____

What could I have done differently today?

_____
_____
_____

True forgiveness is when you can say, Thank you for that experience.
- Oprah Winfrey

CHANGE YOUR BLUEPRINT THROUGH JOURNALING

Date ___/___/_____

Affirmation for today:

My faith is correct; my fear is not.

I am Thankful for...

_____
_____
_____

What would make today great?

_____
_____
_____

What is one act of kindness I can do today?

_____

Awesome things that happened today...

_____
_____
_____

What could I have done differently today?

_____
_____
_____

A good laugh is sunshine in the house.

- William Makepeace Thackeray

CHANGE YOUR BLUEPRINT CHANGE YOUR LIFE

Date ___/___/_____

Affirmation for today:

I am blessed with an incredible family and wonderful friends.

I am Thankful for...

_____
_____
_____

What would make today great?

_____
_____
_____

What is one act of kindness I can do today?

_____

Awesome things that happened today...

_____
_____
_____

What could I have done differently today?

_____
_____
_____

There's power in looking silly and not caring that you do.

- Amy Poehler

CHANGE YOUR BLUEPRINT THROUGH JOURNALING

Date ___/___/_____

Affirmation for today:

I become what I admire in others.

I am Thankful for...

_____
_____
_____

What would make today great?

_____
_____
_____

What is one act of kindness I can do today?

_____

Awesome things that happened today...

_____
_____
_____

What could I have done differently today?

_____
_____
_____

It's hard to beat a person who never gives up.

- Babe Ruth

CHANGE YOUR BLUEPRINT CHANGE YOUR LIFE

Date ___/___/_____

Affirmation for today:
I acknowledge my own self-worth; my confidence is soaring.

I am Thankful for...
_____
_____
_____

What would make today great?
_____
_____
_____

What is one act of kindness I can do today?
_____

Awesome things that happened today...
_____
_____
_____

What could I have done differently today?
_____
_____

All things have been created by the Joyful will of the Infinite Mystery, Life is an experience of making choices about how you want to arrange things in your life. You can choose to arrange things in a Fearful, Egoic way, or you can choose to arrange things in a Loving and Joyful way. When you choose Love and Joy you align with the greatest and highest Good and begin to express your unique creative perspective while at the same time feeling a oneness with everyone else. This will leave you with a feeling of wholeness, joy, peace and gratitude. - Jackson Kiddard

CHANGE YOUR BLUEPRINT THROUGH JOURNALING

Date ___/___/_____

Affirmation for today:

I enjoy wonderful associations with positive, uplifting people.

I am Thankful for...

_____
_____
_____

What would make today great?

_____
_____
_____

What is one act of kindness I can do today?

_____

Awesome things that happened today...

_____
_____
_____

What could I have done differently today?

_____
_____
_____

When people get married because they think it's a long-time love affair, they'll be divorced very soon, because all love affairs end in disappointment. But marriage is a recognition of a spiritual identity.

- Joseph Campbell

CHANGE YOUR BLUEPRINT CHANGE YOUR LIFE

Date ___/___/_____

Affirmation for today:

Everything that is happening now is happening for my ultimate good.

I am Thankful for...

_____
_____
_____

What would make today great?

_____
_____
_____

What is one act of kindness I can do today?

_____

Awesome things that happened today...

_____
_____
_____

What could I have done differently today?

_____
_____
_____

Whatever we are waiting for - peace of mind, contentment, grace, the inner awareness of simple abundance - it will surely come to us, but only when we are ready to receive it with an open and grateful heart.

- Sarah Ban Breathnach

CHANGE YOUR BLUEPRINT THROUGH JOURNALING

Date ___/___/_____

Affirmation for today:

I trust in Love.

I am Thankful for...

_____
_____
_____

What would make today great?

_____
_____
_____

What is one act of kindness I can do today?

_____

Awesome things that happened today...

_____
_____
_____

What could I have done differently today?

_____
_____
_____

I always did something I was a little not ready to do. I think that's how you grow. When there's that moment of 'Wow, I'm not really sure I can do this,' and you push through those moments, that's when you have a breakthrough.

- Marissa Mayer

CHANGE YOUR BLUEPRINT CHANGE YOUR LIFE

Date ___/___/_____

Affirmation for today:

Addiction is teaching me how to love myself. I choose love over pain.

I am Thankful for...

_____
_____
_____

What would make today great?

_____
_____
_____

What is one act of kindness I can do today?

_____

Awesome things that happened today...

_____
_____
_____

What could I have done differently today?

_____
_____
_____

All our final decisions are made in a state of mind that is not going to last.

- Marcel Proust

CHANGE YOUR BLUEPRINT THROUGH JOURNALING

Date ___/___/_____

Affirmation for today:

I am a powerhouse; I am indestructible.

I am Thankful for...
_____
_____
_____

What would make today great?
_____
_____
_____

What is one act of kindness I can do today?
_____

Awesome things that happened today...
_____
_____
_____

What could I have done differently today?
_____
_____
_____

Most of the shadows of this life are caused by our standing in our own sunshine.
- Ralph Waldo Emerson

CHANGE YOUR BLUEPRINT CHANGE YOUR LIFE

Date ___/___/_____

Affirmation for today:

I'm safe as I begin to express myself.

I am Thankful for...

_____
_____
_____

What would make today great?

_____
_____
_____

What is one act of kindness I can do today?

_____

Awesome things that happened today...

_____
_____
_____

What could I have done differently today?

_____
_____
_____

I learned that courage was not the absence of fear, but the triumph over it. The brave man is not he who does not feel afraid, but he who conquers that fear.

- Nelson Mandela

CHANGE YOUR BLUEPRINT THROUGH JOURNALING

Date ___/ ___/ _____

Affirmation for today:

Following my heart and intuition will keep me strong.

I am Thankful for…

_____
_____
_____

What would make today great?

_____
_____
_____

What is one act of kindness I can do today?

_____

Awesome things that happened today…

_____
_____
_____

What could I have done differently today?

_____
_____
_____

Being good in business is the most fascinating kind of art. Making money is art and working is art and good business is the best art.

- Andy Warhol

CHANGE YOUR BLUEPRINT CHANGE YOUR LIFE

Date ___/___/_____

Affirmation for today:

There is no problem so big or so small, that it cannot be solved with love.

I am Thankful for...

_____
_____
_____

What would make today great?

_____
_____
_____

What is one act of kindness I can do today?

_____

Awesome things that happened today...

_____
_____
_____

What could I have done differently today?

_____
_____
_____

Keep away from people who try to belittle your ambitions. Small people always do that, but the really great make you feel that you, too, can become great. When you are seeking to bring big plans to fruition, it is important with whom you regularly associate. Hang out with friends who are like-minded and who are also designing purpose-filled lives. Similarly, be that kind of a friend for your friends.
- Mark Twain

CHANGE YOUR BLUEPRINT THROUGH JOURNALING

Date ___/___/_____

Affirmation for today:

Everyone I come into contact with appreciates me for the wonderful person that I am.

I am Thankful for...

_____
_____
_____

What would make today great?

_____
_____
_____

What is one act of kindness I can do today?

_____

Awesome things that happened today...

_____
_____
_____

What could I have done differently today?

_____
_____
_____

It is one of the beautiful compensations in this life that no one can sincerely try to help another without helping himself.

-Ralph Waldo Emerson

CHANGE YOUR BLUEPRINT CHANGE YOUR LIFE

Date ___/___/_____

Affirmation for today:

I am 100% Self Approved.

I am Thankful for...

_____
_____
_____

What would make today great?

_____
_____
_____

What is one act of kindness I can do today?

_____

Awesome things that happened today...

_____
_____
_____

What could I have done differently today?

_____
_____
_____

When it is obvious that the goals cannot be reached, don't adjust the goals, adjust the action steps.

- Confucius

CHANGE YOUR BLUEPRINT THROUGH JOURNALING

Date ___/___/_____

Affirmation for today:

Life expands as I find the empowering meaning.

I am Thankful for...
_____
_____
_____

What would make today great?
_____
_____
_____

What is one act of kindness I can do today?
_____

Awesome things that happened today...
_____
_____
_____

What could I have done differently today?
_____
_____
_____

We cannot change what we are not aware of, and once we are aware, we cannot help but change.

- Sheryl Sandberg

CHANGE YOUR BLUEPRINT CHANGE YOUR LIFE

Date ___/___/_____

Affirmation for today:

Let's find out what's at the end of this path.

I am Thankful for...

_____
_____
_____

What would make today great?

_____
_____
_____

What is one act of kindness I can do today?

_____

Awesome things that happened today...

_____
_____
_____

What could I have done differently today?

_____
_____
_____

Believe with all of your heart that you will do what you were made to do.

- Orison Swett Marden

CHANGE YOUR BLUEPRINT THROUGH JOURNALING

Date ___/___/_____

Affirmation for today:

Though these times are difficult, they are only a short phase of life.

I am Thankful for...

_____
_____
_____

What would make today great?

_____
_____
_____

What is one act of kindness I can do today?

_____

Awesome things that happened today...

_____
_____
_____

What could I have done differently today?

_____
_____
_____

I think we all wish we could erase some dark times in our lives. But all of life's experiences, bad and good, make you who you are. Erasing any of life's experiences would be a great mistake.

- Luis Miguel

CHANGE YOUR BLUEPRINT CHANGE YOUR LIFE

Date ___/___/_____

Affirmation for today:

My future is an ideal projection of what I envision now.

I am Thankful for...

_____
_____
_____

What would make today great?

_____
_____
_____

What is one act of kindness I can do today?

_____

Awesome things that happened today...

_____
_____
_____

What could I have done differently today?

_____
_____
_____

Freedom is the birthright of every living soul... Thus the inherent nature of man is forever seeking to express itself in terms of freedom. We do well to listen to this Inner Voice, for it tells us of a life wonderful in its scope; of a love beyond our fondest dreams; of a freedom which the soul craves. - Ernest Holmes

CHANGE YOUR BLUEPRINT THROUGH JOURNALING

Date ___/___/_____

Affirmation for today:

I feel the love of those who are not physically around me.

I am Thankful for...

_____
_____
_____

What would make today great?

_____
_____
_____

What is one act of kindness I can do today?

_____

Awesome things that happened today...

_____
_____
_____

What could I have done differently today?

_____
_____
_____

What you seek is seeking you.

-Rumi

CHANGE YOUR BLUEPRINT CHANGE YOUR LIFE

Date ___/___/_____

Affirmation for today:

I look at the beauty life has to offer.

I am Thankful for...

_____
_____
_____

What would make today great?

_____
_____
_____

What is one act of kindness I can do today?

_____

Awesome things that happened today...

_____
_____
_____

What could I have done differently today?

_____
_____
_____

The secret of getting ahead is getting started.

- Mark Twain

CHANGE YOUR BLUEPRINT THROUGH JOURNALING

Date ___/___/_____

Affirmation for today:

My efforts are being supported by the universe; my dreams manifest into reality before my eyes.

I am Thankful for...

_____
_____
_____

What would make today great?

_____
_____
_____

What is one act of kindness I can do today?

_____

Awesome things that happened today...

_____
_____
_____

What could I have done differently today?

_____
_____
_____

Far better it is to dare mighty things, to win glorious triumphs, even though checkered by failure, than to take rank with those poor spirits who neither enjoy nor suffer much, because they live in the gray twilight that knows neither victory nor defeat. - Theodore Roosevelt

CHANGE YOUR BLUEPRINT CHANGE YOUR LIFE

Date ___/___/_____

Affirmation for today:

I celebrate the life of those that I have lost by living mine to the fullest.

I am Thankful for...
_____
_____
_____

What would make today great?
_____
_____
_____

What is one act of kindness I can do today?
_____

Awesome things that happened today...
_____
_____
_____

What could I have done differently today?
_____
_____
_____

Nothing reduces the odds against you like ignoring them.

- Robert Brault

CHANGE YOUR BLUEPRINT THROUGH JOURNALING

Date ___/___/_____

Affirmation for today:

My smile accentuates my beauty.

I am Thankful for...

_____
_____
_____

What would make today great?

_____
_____
_____

What is one act of kindness I can do today?

_____

Awesome things that happened today...

_____
_____
_____

What could I have done differently today?

_____
_____
_____

Letting go doesn't mean that you don't care about someone anymore. It's just realizing that the only person you really have control over is yourself.

- Deborah Reber

CHANGE YOUR BLUEPRINT CHANGE YOUR LIFE

Date ___/___/_____

Affirmation for today:

Love is letting go.

I am Thankful for...

_____
_____
_____

What would make today great?

_____
_____
_____

What is one act of kindness I can do today?

_____

Awesome things that happened today...

_____
_____
_____

What could I have done differently today?

_____
_____
_____

Listen! Clam up your mouth and be silent like an oyster shell, for that tongue of yours is the enemy of the soul, my friend. When the lips are silent, the heart has a hundred tongues.

-Rumi

CHANGE YOUR BLUEPRINT THROUGH JOURNALING

Date ___/___/_____

Affirmation for today:

I radiate beauty, charm, and grace.

I am Thankful for...

_____
_____
_____

What would make today great?

_____
_____
_____

What is one act of kindness I can do today?

_____

Awesome things that happened today...

_____
_____
_____

What could I have done differently today?

_____
_____
_____

When you love someone you don't hurt them on purpose, and cheating on someone isn't a mistake.

- Sonya Parker

CHANGE YOUR BLUEPRINT CHANGE YOUR LIFE

Date ___/___/_____

Affirmation for today:

I am open to life again.

I am Thankful for...

_____
_____
_____

What would make today great?

_____
_____
_____

What is one act of kindness I can do today?

_____

Awesome things that happened today...

_____
_____
_____

What could I have done differently today?

_____
_____
_____

Learning is the beginning of wealth. Learning is the beginning of health. Learning is the beginning of spirituality. Searching and learning is where the miracle process all begins.

- Jim Rohn

CHANGE YOUR BLUEPRINT THROUGH JOURNALING

Date ____/ ____/ _____

Affirmation for today:

I am willing to love everything about myself.

I am Thankful for...

_____
_____
_____

What would make today great?

_____
_____
_____

What is one act of kindness I can do today?

_____

Awesome things that happened today...

_____
_____
_____

What could I have done differently today?

_____
_____
_____

Yesterday I was clever, so I wanted to change the world. Today I am wise, so I am changing myself.

-Rumi

CHANGE YOUR BLUEPRINT CHANGE YOUR LIFE

Date ___/___/_____

Affirmation for today:

My truth is valuable and it's safe for me to come out and share it.

I am Thankful for...

_____
_____
_____

What would make today great?

_____
_____
_____

What is one act of kindness I can do today?

_____

Awesome things that happened today...

_____
_____
_____

What could I have done differently today?

_____
_____
_____

People are always blaming their circumstances for what they are. I don't believe in circumstances. The people who get on in this world are the people who get up and look for the circumstances they want, and, if they can't find them, make them.

- George Bernard Shaw

CHANGE YOUR BLUEPRINT THROUGH JOURNALING

Date ___/___/_____

Affirmation for today:

I am here to solve the problems I see in the world!

I am Thankful for...

_____
_____
_____

What would make today great?

_____
_____
_____

What is one act of kindness I can do today?

_____

Awesome things that happened today...

_____
_____
_____

What could I have done differently today?

_____
_____
_____

What we have done for ourselves alone dies with us; what we have done for others and the world remains and is immortal.

- Albert Pike

www.ingramcontent.com/pod-product-compliance
Lightning Source LLC
Chambersburg PA
CBHW051750040426
42446CB00007B/305